WAR OF THE
VIKINGS™

THE OFFICIAL
GAME GUIDE

By

Aeronwen Trewent, Lisen
&
M Harold Page

paradox
B O O K S™

Pressname: Paradox Books
Copyright © 2014 Paradox Interactive AB

Authors: Aeronwen Trewent, Lisen, M Harold Page
Editor: Tomas Härenstam
Maps: Tobias Tranell
Cover art: Johan Rimér and Love Gunnarsson
ISBN: 978-91-87687-41-9

www.paradoxplaza.com/books

TABLE OF CONTENTS

PART I: THE GAME

CHAPTER 1: THE BASICS

Our first chapter is mainly for those new to the *"War of"* franchise and is an aid to understanding the basic menus, settings and interface for the game in general, and advice on how to make this the best possible game experience. The explanation of the server selection screen will help you to always quickly identify the best available server for your preferred way of playing. The descriptions of the choices available in the settings menu will help you to set up the game to run as smoothly as possible on your computer and to configure the game settings to your preferences.

MAIN MENU CONTROLS

On all menu pages using the "Back" button or the Esc key will return you to the previous screen.

Play Online: Clicking this takes you to a server selection screen, where you have many options to adjust the selection and sorting of the listed servers. To select a server simply click on its name, this will show you who is playing in the server. To enter a server click the 'connect' button at lower right of the screen.

How to Play: Clicking this takes you to an overview of the default controls for mouse and keyboard. There is a lot of information here and these default controls will be referenced later in this Guide.

Tutorial: See Chapter 3 – Fighting.

Loadout Editor: See Chapter 2 – Designing Your Warrior.

Settings: This is where you can adjust the game settings to run as smoothly as possible on your computer and the game controls to suit your play style. For further explanation see below.

Credits: Everyone who has been associated with the making of the game is listed here.

Exit Game: Will exit to desktop.

Server Selection Screen

Across the top of the screen are five tabs:

Internet: Click this to see all servers available.

Favourites: Click this to see all servers you have set as your favourites.

History: Click this to see servers on which you have previously played.

Friends: Click this to see all servers that have recently had a Steam friend of yours playing in them.

LAN: Click this to see all servers on the LAN.

Below this is the table of servers with the following headings (clicking a heading will sort the available servers on that attribute):

Lock Symbol: Indicates a passworded server.

Shield Symbol: Indicates a VAC protected server.

Star Symbol: Indicates a favourite server (click to toggle between a bright star = favourite and dull start = not favourite. Any server with the star highlighted here will appear in the Favourites tab.

Servers: Lists the available servers by name (note the number in brackets indicates the number of available servers).

Gamemode: Indicates which gamemode is currently being played on the server.

Players: Indicates the current number of players (x) and the total number of player slots (y) on that server as x/y.

Person Symbol: Indicates the number of Steam friends of ours on that server.

Map: Indicates which map is currently being played on that server.

Latency: Indicates your calculated ping to the server (often this is strangely high on first entering the server selection screen but shows the true ping on refresh). You will have the best experience if you choose the lowest possible ping.

Clicking on any line for a particular server in this table will pop up a window giving all the details for that server including the steam names of all the players currently in the server. Below the server list are some filter options:

Gamemode: All / Pitched Battle / Arena / Conquest / Team Death Match (TDM).

Map: All / Cliff /Crag / Docks / Forest / Gauntlet / Icefloe/ Monastery / Ravine / Sanctuary / Stronghold / Tide.

Password Protected: Will include password protected servers in the list.

Only Available Servers: Will exclude unavailable servers.

Server not Full: Will show only servers with unallocated player slots.

Server has Player: Will exclude all empty servers.

Below these are three buttons:

Quick refresh: Will only be active when a server is selected and will update the detail screen for that server.

Refresh: Will update the details in the main server list, you have to do this for some of the above filters to take effect.

Connect: Will only be active when a server is selected and will connect to the currently selected server.

SETTINGS

The settings menus can be navigated with the mouse or the keyboard up and down arrow keys. Settings can be toggled with LMB or MMB (RMB acts as a back button). The settings screen has the following options:
- Audio Settings
- Video Settings
- Control Settings
- Key Mapping
- Gameplay Settings

Audio Settings

Master Volume: The master volume will raise or lower the maximum volume for all the other volume settings.

Music Volume: The music does not interfere with gameplay. Have this as loud as is comfortable for you.

SFX Volume: The Sound effects volume affects the audible indicators for gameplay and it is advisable to have this at a high level.

Voice-Over Volume: You will hear the characters making comments appropriate to the game play.

Video Settings

If your game is not running smoothly you may like to lower some of the graphics intensity. The best option is to start with everything on low, alter one setting at a time and play the game for a round or so to determine at what point the game slows down.

Resolution: Has a drop down list of the usual screen resolutions. Higher resolutions will produce sharper images with smoother edges. Having a higher resolution will cause decline in performance, but will also make the game look significantly better. It is preferable to run the game at the native resolution of your monitor.

Gamma: This will change the "brightness" of the game.

Full Screen: This determines whether the game starts in full screen or a windowed mode.

Output Screen: This determines which screen the game should use, if you have several.

Vertical Sync: Briefly, if your game is producing a higher FPS than your monitor can handle you will get "screen tearing". Vsync will "synchronise" the monitor's refresh rate to your graphics card's output. If you have screen tearing issues and you're getting well over 60 FPS on a 60Hz monitor, turn on VSync. If you don't have problems with screen tearing, you might be better turning it off.

Max FPS: This setting is mostly here to avoid overheating some graphics cards as the Bitsquid engine is very efficient in how it loads the GPU so it can give some cards issues. Set this to "no" unless you have an overheating graphics card.

Max Stacking Frames: This determines how many "frames" of video that the game allows the graphics card drivers to buffer before rendering them. Essentially, if you have a higher amount or auto the drivers will give you a smoother framerate but they will also introduce input lag as it will be showing you "old" frames

Graphics Quality: Changing to Low, Medium or High will apply presets to all the video options below this point.

Shadow Quality: This determines the level of detail of shadows. If you have problems with the game this is the first setting to lower.

Character/Environment Textures: Lower resolution textures will look blurry or dull, and high resolution textures will look sharp and lifelike. Texture quality is unlikely to affect your frame rate but it does require more video Ram so you may experience more intermittent stuttering. Raise textures as high as you can without the game stuttering. If you get the occasional pause, lower this setting until the stutter goes away.

Shield Textures: As above.

Anti-Aliasing: FXAA stands for Fast Approximate Anti-Aliasing. It aims to reduce jagged edges around objects. It uses a method of doing so which requires almost no processing power but looks a bit blurrier. If jagged edges annoy you more than blurriness try FXAA.

LOD: Level of Detail, how accurately distant objects are portrayed. A lower setting will mean objects will switch to their lower rez versions earlier. Can be CPU intensive, set low if you are having FPS issues.

Terrain Decoration Density: This determines how much detail will display on the ground. This does not affect much in game and can be set to low.

Scatter Density: This defines how much scenery (vegetation) is added. This does not affect much in game and can be set to low if you have any performance issues.

Particles Quality: This determines how the particle based effects in the game display (e.g. smoke, blood splatter). This does not affect much in game and can be set to low if you have any performance issues.

Light Casts Shadows: This determines whether secondary light sources (not the sun) like torches etc. should cast shadows. This setting can have a significant impact on the game's performance. If you have problems with the game this is the first setting to lower.

SSAO: Screen Space Ambient Occlusion, determines how ambient lighting generates shadows. Can have a major impact on frame rate. If you are struggling for FPS turn this off.

Cloth Quality: This determines how the cloak movement is displayed. If you set it to off it won't use cloth simulation at all, just use pre-animated cloaks.

Control Settings

Mouse Sensitivity: This setting makes the cursor move faster or slower than its CPI for melee. Adjust to your play style.

Aim Sensitivity Modifier: This makes the cursor move faster or slower than its CPI for archery aiming. Adjust to your play style.

Invert Mouse Look: This allows the user to look downward by moving the mouse forward and upward by moving the mouse backward.

Parry with Keyboard: Keyboard movement keys combined with RMB determines parry the direction.

Attack with Keyboard: Keyboard movement keys combined with LMB determines attack the direction.

Invert Swing X-Axis, Invert Swing Y-Axis, Invert Parry X-Axis, Invert Parry Y-Axis: These four controls simply reverse the mouse movement direction needed to swing and parry.

Double-Tap to Dodge: With this set double tapping a direction button (WASD) will cause dodge.

Travel Mode Input Type: With this set to "Hold" the Travel Mode key must be held down to enter and remain in Travel Mode. With this set to "Toggle" the Travel Mode key must be clicked to enter and to leave Travel Mode. With this set to "Flexible" either option will work for your Travel Mode key.

Key Mapping: This will take you to another screen with the game control keys listed (scroll down to see all options). Click the action you would like to change the key for and the key designation will start blinking. Simply press the key you would like to designate for that action. If you are happy with the changes click "Apply Settings". If you would like to revert to the defaults click "reset".

Gameplay settings

Crosshair: Simply select the type you prefer.

Crosshair Opacity: Determines how clearly the crosshair is displayed, at the lowest setting the crosshair is transparent and you cannot see it.

Crosshair Red / Crosshair Green / Crosshair Blue: Determines the colour of the cross hair, with all three at maximum setting the crosshair is white and with all three at the lowest setting the crosshair is black. Experiment to find the best setting for each map.

Show HUD: If this is set to "off" none of the other features in this menu are shown, nor are the Stamina and charge bar, the perk icons etc.

Show Combat Text: This is text that pops up next to characters giving you information for example if you hit a character with the Juggernaut perk while he is in Travel Mode combat text will explain why he did not trip.

Show XP Rewards: Shows the amount of XP you get for each rewarded action.

Show Parry Helper: With this set you get an orange arc in the direction an enemy near you is attacking, a blue arc in the direction in which you are parrying.

Show Charge Helper: The bar on the HUD showing how charged your swing is.

Show Announcements: Announcements state kill streaks, changes to the state of Objective points, etc.

Show Teammate Outlines: Teammates are outlined in blue.

Show Squad Outlines: Squad members are outlined in green. Read about squads in Chapter 4.

Show Tagged Enemy Outlines: Pressing T while looking at an enemy gives them a red outline seen by all members of the same squad.

Hide Blood: If this is set you will not see the blood on weapons, blood on the ground and blood on the characters.

Hide Squads in Scoreboard: If this is on players are not listed by squad but by score. If this is off, squads are listed by highest scoring squad.

Auto Join Squad: If this is on you are automatically placed in the first available squad with the most players.

MAIN SCREEN HUD

The lower edge of the screen has a bar with the following components:

At each end a pearl in a dragon's mouth indicates your current level (left) and your next level (right). The narrow bar between them has in indicator showing your progress between the two levels.

Of the three round icons on the left, two indicate when you are in a squad and whether you are near squad members. The third icon is reserved for future use.

The two bars indicate your Stamina (top and fawn) and your Health (bottom and green).

The four round icons on the right indicate your perks. They will glow when a perk is activated and for some perks will indicate the recharge time.

Text Chat

The text chat will scroll on the lower left of the screen.

Y will open the chat bar with the /say command ready. This chat will be seen by all players and will be prefixed [Team].

U will open the chat bar with the /say_team command ready. This chat will be seen by all players and will be prefixed [All].

Enter will open chat in the last mode in which it was opened. Enter will also work to open chat between rounds.

The Kill Feed

The kill feed scrolls in the upper right. When a character is knocked down the kill feed shows *Killer's Name > Weapon Icon > Name of the Killed Player*. Player names are always their current Steam name. Names in the kill feed are coloured blue for your own team, green for squad mates and red for opponents.

If a character is killed by a fall or drowning the kill is attributed to the last player to have caused them damage, unless that player has left the server. If no other player has caused the dead player any damage the death is listed in the kill feed as a self-kill. Sometimes the kill feed shows no killer.

This all has the rather strange consequence that you can be credited with a kill even when you are nowhere near the player who died, or if that player killed you but then fell off a cliff or stepped into water.

The Centre Top

The centre top of the screen has a round timer and game mode specific information. Other information (e.g. combat text) pops up onto the screen as appropriate.

INTERACTING WITH OTHER PLAYERS

In any online PvP game, your in-game experience and that of those around you can be enhanced by treating other players respectfully. If you are friendly most people will respond in kind and you will have a new community of friends.

Remember that players from all over the world, of all ages, both genders have come together to play the same game. This means that you have the common experience of playing the game with everyone you meet.

A good rule of thumb is to watch your language. Be practical and avoid foul language or any terms that have negative connotations relating to racial descriptions, sexual orientation or gender. The text chat from other players can be read on the lower left hand side of the screen.

Here are some general guidelines that can help you make the most of your in game interactions with other people:

- Remember that when in a PvP game not everyone sees the in game chat all the time. Most people will respond if they see the chat.
- If your chat is directed at one player use their name so that they and other players on the server know to whom you are speaking.
- If you do not understand something, ask someone openly and deferentially.
- If you accidentally hit or kill a teammate, apologies go a long way to smoothing ruffled feelings.
- Remember that game modes and server settings can differ. If a player is clearly unaware of the details of this server enlighten them politely.
- When you see someone playing well assume they are skilled (not that they have some hack).
- When you are bested by another player compliment them on their skill.
- Trash talking can be fun between good friends but is easily misunderstood as hostility by others. Make it clear that you are referring to your friend if you must use in game chat.
- If you can't say anything nice do not say anything at all.

CHAPTER 2: DESIGNING YOUR WARRIOR

This chapter introduces the profile editor and explains which choices are available and how they will affect your fighting style. We feel that your own exploration and inventiveness is better than an in depth discussion of cosmetic items. However, the different martial choices are discussed, and the ramifications of each choice indicated. "It matters little how much equipment we use; it matters much that we be masters of all we do use."

PREMADE PROFILES

The character you play can be one of two types: a premade profile – with the look, weapons and perks already determined and which you cannot alter – or a custom profile with all aspects of the character available for you to select from the options you have so far unlocked on your account.

Initially only the premade profiles are available, but customisable profile slots will become available as coins and XP are gained. Progress though the initial premade classes to obtaining a customisable profile slot is designed to familiarise the player with the basics of the game and is expected to be quite rapid.

In the Loadout Editor for each custom slot that you have unlocked you will be able to select all aspects of your warrior's profile – both those which affect gameplay (martial options) and those which do not (cosmetic options). As you progress with XP and coins more custom profile slots become available for you to design warriors to suit your play style. Coins and XP are account wide. Weapons, perks and taunts need to be unlocked once only. Cloaks, beards and heads need to be unlocked per team. Helmets and armour patterns need to be unlocked per class and team.

Of the customisable options only the weapons and perks will affect your performance. Armour is not customisable but does differ in effect for each of the classes. All other options (helmets etc.) are purely cosmetic.

The list below describes the weapons and perk for each of the three default class profiles:

Skirmisher

Primary Weapon: *Longbow*
Secondary Weapon: *One-Handed Axe*
Perk 1: *Skirmisher*
Perk 2: *Quick Blood*
Perk 3: *Eagle Eye*
Perk 4: *Strong Arm*

Warrior

Primary Weapon: *Sword*
Secondary Weapon: *Throwing Axe*
Shield: *Round*
Perk 1: *Jack of all Trades*
Perk 2: *Agile Fighter*

Perk 3: *Adrenaline Rush*
Perk 4: *Chaser*

Champion

Primary Weapon: *Two-Handed Axe*
Secondary Weapon: *Throwing Daggers*
Perk 1: *Stubborn*
Perk 2: *Brawler*
Perk 3: *Agile Fighter*
Perk 4: *Hard Hitter*

THE LOADOUT EDITOR

The Loadout Editor contains the menus for selecting all aspects of your custom profiles. When clicking "Loadout Editor" in the main menu you are taken to the Profile Selection Page. Here (when you have obtained one or more custom profile slots) you can select a profile to customise or enter the Shield Paint Editor. At any point you can also select between the Viking and Saxon "look" of the profile by clicking the Mjolnir or Cross icon. As you cycle through the custom profiles available you will see the current weapons and perks allocated to each profile.

The Loadout Screen

On selection of a profile to customise, you enter the Loadout Screen. It is possible to cycle through the profiles available for customisation at the top centre of the screen. Here you can also name your custom profiles by simply typing over the profile name. On the left are the options for martial items, on the right options for cosmetic items and the Viking/Saxon toggle. In the centre you can see the character you create (the view of the character can be

rotated by holding LMB while moving the mouse). Information about your level, XP and coins available is on the centre of the screen below the character.

Cosmetic Options

The cosmetic customisable options available are:
- Helmet
- Patterns
- Face
- Heads
- Cloaks
- Beards
- Taunts (press R to use in game)
- Shield Design

Try out the options until you have created the character you want. Vikings generally have "cool" colours and Saxons have "warm" colours. Customisable options become available in "tiers" depending on XP.

21

Martial Options

Begin by selecting the class you wish to play. The class determines the armour level (and look) of the character, and also which perks are locked for the character. Each class has four perk slots (of which one or two have perks preselected for that class). Perks locked by class are those in the first and second perk slots that cannot be changed.

There are currently three classes to choose from: *Skirmisher, Warrior* and *Champion*.

The Skirmisher has cloth armour with little protection, which means it can only absorb a few hits before being knocked down. The locked perks make the Skirmisher perfect for standing back and shooting.

The Warrior has medium armour which means it can last a bit longer in the thick of battle. The Warrior has only one locked perk slot, which makes it the best choice if you wish to have the most perk options.

The Champion has heavy armour which is made for surviving in the thick of battle. The Champion is a great class for being engaged in melee a lot, dealing and absorbing a lot of damage.

Unlocked perk slots can be filled with the perk of your choice, selected from the drop down menu. Note you cannot select the same perk twice, nor will the class restricted perks be available in the drop down menu. The locked perks and armour level for each class are:

Skirmisher

Armour level: *Low*
Perk 1: *Skirmisher*
Perk 2: *Quick Blood*

Warrior

Armour level: *Medium*
Perk 1: *Jack of all Trades*

Champion

Armour level: *High*
Perk 1: *Stubborn*
Perk 2: *Brawler*

Once you have selected the class the weapons available to that class in each of the slots are available for selection. Weapon types that are available for both the primary and the secondary slot are greyed out in one slot if chosen for the other.

PERKS

This section gives an explanation of each perk, the benefits it gives and helpful information about the use of the perk.

All profiles have four perks. Each class has one or two class perks that are locked, i.e. cannot be changed for that class type. Class perks cannot be used for other classes.

Some perks are passive and others are active. Active perks can be initiated by one of the perk keys Z, X, C or V. When a perk is activated it will light up in the perk icon on the information bar at the lower edge of the screen. When a perk has a cooldown the icon will gradually revert to the unlit state, indicating the cooldown time.

Skirmisher Class Perks

Skirmisher: Light Armour gives 13% damage reduction. Deals 33% extra headshot damage. 30% reduced Stamina cost for firing arrows. Weapon swapping 25% faster.

Tips: This is a perk you want if you want to shoot a lot and avoid melee. The damage reduction is very low but the bonuses for shots are big. Gives you a quite high rate of fire.

Quick Blood: No Stamina cost for jumping. Doubled Stamina regeneration while in Travel Mode.

Tips: When you have depleted your Stamina by shooting, quickly go into Travel Mode and change location, this will regenerate your Stamina quickly. Even just a short distance is enough to get full Stamina.

Warrior Class Perks

Jack of All Trades: Medium armour gives 30% damage reduction. Both weapon slots counts as primary.

Champion Class Perks

Stubborn: Heavy armour gives 40% damage reduction. Stamina regeneration reduced by 10%.

Brawler: Your swings and parries and blocks are not interrupted by ranged weapons. Special attacks destroy shield if blocked.

Tips: With Brawler you can easily take out your enemies' shields by using any of the special attacks. Then you can use your throwing weapons on them and they will not be able to cover behind their shield. This is also greatly helping your own team's archers.

Pickable Perks

Blade Master: Successful parries give a faster side step.

Tips: If you feel comfortable in parrying this perk lets you play in a way that rely a lot on parrying and not so much on footwork. You can hold ground by parrying and every parry make you regain a small amount of Health if you have lost any. If you have spent most of your Stamina by attacking you can play defensively and parry to regain Stamina.

Adrenaline Rush: Killing an enemy instantly refills your Stamina bar.
Tips: If you want to be effective while fighting many at once, this is a good perk. You don't have to worry about spending all your Stamina on killing 1 opponent, as it will refill your Stamina to 100% when you succeed letting you move on to next opponent.

Agile Fighter: Allows you to perform an attack while dodging by pressing LMB.
Tips: If you look for it, there is often a time window after you back-dodge were you can hit back, while your opponent recovers a missed attack. You can also quickly dodge forward to damage or kill opponents that try to walk away from you.

Blind Fury: You can throw any of the melee weapons (not a dagger).
Tips: This can be a good perk in Conquest where a lot of weapons lie around on contested Objective points.

Blood Thirst: Killing an enemy regenerates 5% Health each second for 5 seconds.
Tips: If you see a squad member on low Health and you know they have blood thirst you can assist them by letting them deal the killing blow on your enemies so they can recover. If you want to focus on getting many kills this is a great perk because you don't have to bandage so often if you actually manage to get the kills.

Chaser: Grants 20% increased movement speed when chasing enemies from behind. Increases tackle radius by 20%.
Tips: This perk is very useful in the Conquest game mode if you want to play defensively and are able to spot opponents that try to sneak around parts of the map to get to

your held Objective. You will be able to catch up to them and tackle them using E when close enough.

Dodge Block: Gives you the ability to dodge while blocking with a shield.
Tips: This is a good perk for the defensive kind of player, it lets you hold a block up if you need to dodge in any direction. You can use it to dodge block in front of a teammate that needs assistance, either by catching projectiles or melee blows.

No Perk: Reduces your combat potential and boosts enemy efficiency by 27%. If you want to feel special by having a disadvantage this is a "no perk" for you.

Eagle Eye: Gives you a zoom when aiming with a bow. Hits at a distance of 46 yards or more give extra damage.
Tips: This perk will make you able to zoom in, making long distances matter less. It is a great perk if you want to play the kind of archer who stand far back away from the actual fighting, sniping other archers. You can also use it at closer range making precise shots hitting enemies who fight your teammates.

Feign Death: Press perk key to feign death. Your character falls over with a random death animation as if he was knocked down but displays no finish off icon. After two seconds, if you try to move or press the perk button, you stand back up again.
Tips: If you have nowhere to hide from ranged attacks but some low objects that are still too tall to cover you if you crouch, feign death can be used for being in cover. If you are standing near a non-fatal drop you can feign death and fall out of sight to evade attack.

Flaming Arrow: Sets enemy shields ablaze for 10 seconds. Two flaming arrows striking a shield in quick succession destroy the shield.

Tips: Because you have 10 seconds to hit a shield again, a quicker kind of bow might be of more use with this perk.

Gloater: Full Health is restored after successfully taunting an enemy close by. Pressing the perk key initiates a special taunt. You can't voluntarily abort the taunt, but it will be interrupted if hit.

Hard Hitter: You can hold a fully charged melee swing five times longer than normal. Fully charged swings damaging an enemy target makes the next swing charge 50 % faster (note that this does not affect the minimum pose time of the weapon).
Tips: This perk lets you hold charged swings up for a long time which makes it very good for group fights. Take your time with a fully charged charge bar and find targets who are busy fighting your teammates.

Juggernaut: You are not knocked down by enemy attacks whilst sprinting.
Tips: If you come across an enemy team with a lot of archers, Juggernaut is perfect for letting you use Travel Mode until you reach attacking distance. It is also a good perk to have as you don't have to worry about using Travel Mode as means to moving around most of the time.

Niding: Allows you to backstab enemies when wielding a dagger. Your footsteps are inaudible.
Tips: If you sneak up on enemies while you have your dagger out they will not hear you, but if you want to change to other weapons that will give you away. With dagger out you can kick, which is useful if your opponent is standing close to a cliff or water.

Spotter: Ranged attacks which hit or pass close to an enemy target will automatically mark that target for the rest of the squad. You can see Health and Stamina bars on marked enemies.

Tips: Very useful on smaller maps and in game mode Arena where it is important that your team focus on the same target at times. If you manage to hit and damage opponents, your squad members will be able to make a decision to go after that target based on what they see.

Strong Arm: Bows stay fully charged for 5 times as long. Fully charged shots can pierce enemies and hit up to two targets. *Tips:* If you want to make few but powerful shots this is a good perk for you. You also have plenty of time to aim with this perk.

Strong Will: When you get knocked down, you will start reviving yourself after five seconds. Until you start reviving herself, instead of the revive icon, your teammates see the perk icon above your downed body. The auto-revive can be interrupted like any other revive, but you will immediately start getting up again if interrupted, until finished off in the normal way.
Tips: If you play archer and stray away from your team in order to outflank the enemy team, you don't have to worry if you get knocked down, this perk will let you get up again.

Sure Shot: If you hit a target with an arrow the next arrow will charge 50% faster. The effect lasts five seconds.
Tips: If you shooting is easy for you and you manage to hit with most arrows, this perk let you have a very high rate of fire. The perk's effectiveness depends on how accurate you are.

WEAPON TYPES

This section is a brief note about the weapon types in the game to help you decide which you would prefer to have in your profile. Within each weapon type the weapons have the same performance, just different appearance.

Every melee weapon type has a special attack. These are explained in detail in Chapter 3.

One-Handed Sword

The one-handed sword can hit through more than one player. You need to be careful using a sword close to teammates, because even if you hit enemies the blade will go through their bodies and possibly hit one of your teammates.

Because the sword can hit through several opponents it can be very useful if you fight many at once. If your opponents move too close together your swings can pass through and hit all of them.

The sword has a quite long range. It is a good choice if you want to rely on foot work – the long range makes it easier to let players with shorter weapons swing and miss, while you, if careful enough, have the range to hit them instead.

The sword is also great for fighting players who use shields. The sword has a quite "thin" hit box which makes it easy to hit places on opponents which are not completely covered with the shield. Even if just a small part of the legs or tip of the head is not covered, you can hit those parts with the sword if you get the angles right.

A one-handed sword can be used with a shield.

Special Attack: Thrust

One-Handed Axe

The one-handed axe deals a little more damage than the sword but cannot hit through several opponents. The one-handed axe is good if you play in tight formations and close to teammates because if you hit an opponent the axe will not go through your opponent and hit teammates.

29

The high damage is also helpful if you play close to teammates as you can give the charge bar time to charge up and hit for good amounts of damage.

The one-handed axe can be used together with a shield.

Special Attack: Side Swing

Dagger

Daggers don't deal as much damage as the other one-handed weapons and are quite short. It is however useful in small spaces when the room to swing weapons is limited.

Special Attack: Kick

Two-Handed Axe

The two-handed axe is very powerful if you manage the charge bar and let it be full or close to full. If you connect a hit, depending on what armour your opponent is wearing, you will often deal close to 100 damage.

The two-handed axe is also the easiest weapon to make instant kills with. Instantly killed players can't be revived.

Quick hits from two-handed axes (quick hits are hits you just mouse-click and release without charging the charge bar) deal about as much as the quick hits from the one-handed weapons. The two-handed axe relies more on the charge bar than the other weapons do. So if you play against players who are good at blocking and parrying it might only be useful if you are able to catch them off guard.

Special Attack: Overhead Swing

Spear

The spear has quite a quick attack and decent range making it useful for group fights where you want to hit opponents that do not see it coming. The spear's special attack is a powerful push rather than an actual attack with the weapon. This is useful in duels (1vs1). If your opponent gets in close to you, push is a good way to gain distance. When you push someone you can, if you are quick enough, have time to hit them before they can block or parry.

Push is also what makes the spear useful in group fights because if you push enemies, your teammates will have time to hit and damage them.

You can also use the spear's push ability to push opponents off bridges or other high grounds.

Special Attack: Push

Throwing Dagger

The throwing dagger does not deal so much damage but they fly quite straight making them easy to hit with. They are useful for interrupting enemies bandaging or hitting people in Travel Mode hoping to trip them over.

If you carefully observe how much damage your enemies are taking, the throwing knives can help you kill off weak enemies who are close to death.

Throwing Axe

The throwing axes deal medium damage and they are very useful to start a fight with. If you make one throwing axe hit, you will often not have to deal so much more damage in melee until you have secured the kill.

Javelin

The javelin generally deals a big amount of damage. If you hit someone with a javelin they will often then be close to death. If you hit someone in the head it will be an instant kill.

The javelin can be a bit tricky to hit with because when you start the throw it takes a little time before it releases.

Javelins will break shields if you hit them. Be careful not to hit your teammates' shields.

Shields

A shield lets you block an incoming attack if you manage to move the shield to meet it. Shields are great if you want to play the supporting role. It is great for covering bandaging teammates from incoming projectiles or to help you revive teammates by covering them while they get on their feet.

If you get into an area with a lot of opponents shooting or throwing weapons at you, remember that you can put your shield on your back. It can also be very useful to have the shield on your back while you fight enemies in melee because enemy archers will have a hard time hitting you.

Longbow

The longbow has a fairly flat arc and therefore hits the target quite fast. This bow is for longer range shots. Use with the Skirmisher whose lighter armour needs more distance from the melee. With long distance you can take other archers unawares. When you have a stationary target (archer shooting or player bandaging) go for the headshot.

Hunting Bow

The Hunting bow is a fast bow but has a big drop and is therefore better at a closer range. Over a long range you have to aim quite a way above the target and the arrow takes so long to arrive that your target has had time to have a cup of tea, a piece of cake and amble away before it arrives. The damage is lower than for a longbow but the fire rate is faster. Use with a Warrior for the extra armour protection as you will be nearer the melee.

XP AND COINS

In the game you can earn Experience Points (XP) and coins. XP is gained through in-game actions. Examples:

- Instant Kill: 150
- Enemy Kill within Objective: 10
- Enemy Knockdown: 100
- Execution: 200
- Finish Off: 50
- Headshot: 100
- Longshot: 25
- Objective Captured: 250
- Revive: 200
- Using a Perk: variable

Coins are gained through time playing in game. At the end of a round (whether or not you are still on the server) you receive the coins appropriate to the time played. Idling in game will not gain coins.

The amount of coins you gain per minute can be increased by gaining *renown*. The higher level of renown you have the higher the coin per minute multiplier. The XP bar shows your current level of XP as a brown line and the amount of XP you need to get to the next renown level as a blue line. On entering a map a small pop up shows the renown level you have reached, the amount of XP you need to obtain in order to reach the next renown level and the time you have left to reach it. If you do not reach the next renown level in time your renown is reset to 0.

Coins can also be bought via the customisation panel. Buying coins will make the in-game items more accessible to those that do not have a lot of time to spend in game. The XP requirements remain, however.

Using XP and Coins

As you gain XP you will gain in-game levels. At certain levels in-game items will become available to you to buy with your in-game coins. The items are released in tiers. Most higher tier and higher cost items will have cosmetic differences but the same stats as easily accessible items.

CHAPTER 3: FIGHTING

In this chapter we discuss the specifics about the games internal systems. Learn how to strike, parry, block, shoot, dodge and launch a special attack. While this guide is mainly intended for beginners we expect that more experienced players will find some interesting information and food for thought here. It is an intricate chapter and a primer on how to kill, and stay alive, while playing the game. The key to making the most of the advice here is to practice each element, no skill worth gaining was ever gained without effort.

The tutorial: There is a tutorial in the game, which will help you master the basic concepts. Later in this chapter is section on how to make the most of the tutorial.

MELEE

This section of the guide will cover the basics of fighting in close combat. It will teach you how to strike, parry, and use your weapons' special attacks.

Striking

There are three basic strikes in the game. To strike, use you left mouse button while moving the mouse in a certain direction.

Overhead Swing: Use LMB while moving the mouse forward to make an overhead attack.

Left Swing: Use LMB while moving the mouse left to make a left swing.

Right Swing: Use LMB while moving the mouse right to make a right swing.

When making a swing, hold the LMB to charge the attack and release the LMB to make the attack. As you charge an attack the charge bar will appear and will quickly fill from left to right. The more the charge bar is filled the more damage the attack will do.

However, after reaching full charge the charge will quickly deplete back to the initial charge. As the charge bar fills there is a distinctive sound, therefore without checking the visual indicator you can always know the point at which the charge bar is full and your swing will do the most damage.

You will still do some damage when the charge bar is not full, though with slower swings and less damage than with fully loaded charges. Ensure that you recognise and listen for the charge sound when you practice.

Stamina: At the lower edge of the screen is the light grey Stamina bar, and below that, the green Health bar. With each attack the Stamina bar is depleted by a set amount, this amount is the same no matter how charged the attack. The Stamina bar replenishes over time. Repeated quick attacks will cause the Stamina bar to deplete faster than it can replenish.

If you do not have enough Stamina for an attack the attack will not be made and you will hear a "clonk" sound. As the Stamina bar gets below 50% you will grunt as you strike, sounding more tired. Ensure that you are familiar with all these audible cues.

Parrying

There are three basic parries. To parry, use you right mouse button while moving the mouse in a certain direction.

Overhead Parry: Use RMB while moving the mouse forward to parry an overhead attack.

Left Parry: Use RMB while moving the mouse left to parry an attack on your left.

Right Parry: Use RMB while moving the mouse right to parry an attack on your right.

A parry will stop any attack as long as your weapon is between you and your opponent's weapon. For instance a left parry will normally stop a right attack, but if positioned correctly it will also stop a left attack. If you successfully parry, your next attack will be faster than normal and will charge faster than normal.

As the blade of the enemy hits your blade you will hear the collision. When you hear that sound you are safe to begin your next parry or strike.

If you fail to parry and are hit you character will flinch and you will see some blood. Be aware that if someone connects with a hit their next hit will come more quickly.

The Parry Helper: The parry helper shows an orange arc in the direction someone is about to strike and a blue arc (briefly black) in the direction you are actually parrying. Parry helpers are considered as cheats by most experienced players and this is why they have no place in the competitive scene. We recommend that you turn off the parry helpers and use the tutorial without them.

Special Attacks

All melee weapons have a special attack, which can be performed by pressing F. This will put your character into an attack animation that you cannot interrupt (but can steer a little). Special attacks use about 25% of your Stamina, so be careful of trying to do too many in quick succession. The one-handed sword, the one-handed axe, the two-handed axe, the dagger and the spear all have different special attacks.

The One-Handed Sword has a medium ranged thrust attack which cannot be parried, only blocked with a shield. Be aware of parts of your opponent's body that are not protected by the shield, if he holds the shield low, aim for the head. Or if he is holding the shield high go for his legs.

The One-Handed Axe has more of an area of effect-like special attack which cannot be parried, it can however be blocked with a shield. As the one-handed axe special attack affects players on your side it is not so useful if you fight close to teammates when friendly fire is on. If you have enemies around you and cannot escape, the one-handed axe special might, if you are lucky, hit and kill several opponents.

The Two-Handed Axe has a long range special attack. The special is an overhead attack so this special is, as the one-handed sword special, still an option while having teammates close to you. If it lands this will almost always instantly kill unless you hit the legs or feet. This special attack is tricky to land if the opponent gets too close and/or moves around a lot. It is very good to use against players who use special attacks and miss, or against players who dodge, you might still be able to catch them with the two-handed axe's long range.

The Dagger has a *kick* as a special attack. The kick connects directly forward so needs to be aimed carefully. A successful kick will cause the opponent to move about three metres backwards, this means it is most successful on the edges of high places where it can cause the opponent a fatal fall. However the kicking player also moves forward about a metre during the animation and therefore care must be taken not to kick when too close to cliffs etc. An opponent who dodges a kick has enough time to line up and kick at the attacker; this can also make the kick a dangerous option on cliff edges. The kick does no damage, just leaves the kicked player helpless for about 2 seconds.

The Spear has a *push* as a special attack. The push has an area of effect almost as wide as the spear so when facing several opponents it can give a breathing space to deal with them. Otherwise the spear push pushes the opponent backwards far enough to give space to use the spear thrust. The push causes a stagger long enough that you can repeatedly push an opponent while your Stamina lasts. As with the dagger kick, this special can be very effective at the edges of high places. As with the kick the push itself does no damage.

After executing a special attack you will be vulnerable for a short time. This means that in a duel if you miss, your opponent has time to deal damage to you, either by attacking you until you can recover, or by performing a special attack on their own.

Some players (often new players) tend to overuse the special attack. If you have either of the one-handed weapons your reach is limited and you will have to be extra careful facing a two-handed axe special-attack trigger happy player. You might have to dodge and keep your distance and wait for the other player's Stamina to get low, before you want to go in and try to damage him. If you come across a one-handed weapon special attack-spammer while you have the two-handed axe, you have the range advantage and you can feint to move closer and hope they will trigger their special attack, when they do this, if you have been careful enough, they will not have the range to hit you but you will hit them with your special, as you have the longer range.

When you parry an opponent try to land a special attack right after. It can be easier to land the special after parry if you are using the sword. Some opponents move around a lot all the time so risking a special after parry might not be worth it, but if someone plays quite a static manner or the environment does not let them move around much, you should consider doing a special attack right after parry.

How to Self-Train: With your chosen weapon play some games where your only attack is the special. You are likely to die a lot, do not let this deter you. Keep doing this until you know you are in control of where and when to hit an opponent. You will quickly get a feel for the range and direction of the special, but also for how your opponents can strike while you are in the animation. When you are completely comfortable that you know which times a special will get you killed and when it will kill an opponent put this to the test by mixing it in with normal attacks.

The Shield

If you have a shield, pressing 4 will take out or put away your shield. While holding a shield, holding RMB will put your shield in a defensive position. Your shield will block any incoming attack for which the shield is directly between you and a weapon whether or not you have it in hand. When holding RMB to block with your shield, you must aim your shield at the weapon not at the other player. The shield protects only the area it covers and a hit around the side, above or below the shield will damage you.

When blocking with a shield you lose Stamina each

time it is hit. When your Stamina reaches zero your shield will drop. You can loot your shield again (or any other) when you have regained some Stamina. While holding a shield in a defensive position you regain Stamina more slowly than if you were not holding the shield.

A shield will protect from a sword or one-handed axe special attack. However if your shield is hit by a two-handed axe special attack your shield will drop and will not be retrievable. Shields are also destroyed by javelins.

You can hold your shield in a defensive position while crouching, and some players like to walk up to an archer this way. Be aware however that while crouching you move very slowly and it is easy for an archer to shoot at your slow moving, exposed legs.

Target Selection

If you are engaged in a melee your immediate target is obviously that opponent. However, if a teammate is also engaged nearby, you can often manoeuvre so that you are also within strike range of your teammate's opponent and make an unanticipated hit.

If you are unengaged, look for where you can help a teammate in a fight, especially where you can outnumber the opponents. Or if an engaged teammate is being targeted by an archer, try to get the archer. Even threatening the archer is helpful as when the archer has to take evasive action or switches to shooting you, your engaged teammate can concentrate on his melee fight.

When selecting targets, always weigh the risk against the reward. For example, when you sneak up on an unwary archer with no other opponents around, an attack is low risk and high reward but if you attack an opponent who is bandaging it is possible he is faking to lure your attack, and this is a higher risk for the same reward.

RANGED COMBAT

Hold your right mouse button to charge and aim a shot and press your left mouse button to release. As you press RMB and raise the bow your character will go into first person view and remain there until you release the RMB. When you have made the shot you can continue to hold the RMB and your character will reload the bow and the next shot will charge.

As you charge the shot the charge bar will fill, when the charge bar is full it will pause there briefly and then will oscillate between about 2/3 full and full, at the same time the arrow will shake slightly. Do not let of these things disturb your shot, hold the bow and release when the shot is aimed.

As the charge bar fills there is a distinctive sound. The sound that happens when the charge bar is full repeats as the bar oscillates, therefore without checking the visual indicator you can always know the point at which the charge bar is full and your shot will do the most damage. However you will still do some damage when the charge bar is not full, so do not worry about that too much it is more important to hit your target than to fire at full charge.

The lower third of the charge bar is coloured blue, while the shot is charging through this part of the bar releasing the LMB will result in a clunking sound and no arrow is fired. However this failed shot will still consume Stamina.

With each shot the Stamina bar is depleted by a set amount, this amount is the same no matter how charged the attack is. At a certain low level of Stamina you can no longer raise the bow for a shot, and you will be ejected from first person view even though you are still holding the RMB. If your Stamina is low you cannot raise your bow and therefore, cannot shoot. The audible cue is that your character will breathe heavily. However the charge bar refills quickly and so this is a momentary interruption.

Damage

The damage done by your shot depends on where it hits the opponent and what bow you use. A rule of thumb is: For the same charge a shot does more damage the higher it hits.

Fully charged headshots from a longbow, hitting either flesh or helm, will kill instantly. But so may a low charged shot. Fully charged headshots from a hunting bow will not kill instantly.

With the Strong Arm perk a fully charged shot will go through the target and hit whatever is behind. If this piercing shot hits another player it will damage them and the shooter will get a multiple hit bonus. The arrow will not go through the second player to hit a third.

Aim

While actual distances depend upon which bow is being used, generally for closer shots you aim exactly where you want to hit but for longer shots you aim slightly above where you want to hit. For very long shots you aim considerably above where you want to hit.

Moving Targets: For longer shots be aware that the time taken for the arrow to reach the target will also be longer, so you may also need to allow for the opponents movement in that time as well as for the distance. When shooting a moving target the aim should be in front of the target so that they move into the aim as the arrow reaches the target.

When aiming at an erratically moving target, for example one that is fighting, keep your bow still in an area they are likely to move into and fire when the target is in position, rather than trying to follow their movement with the bow.

Shooting into Melee: The best advice for shooting into a melee fight is "don't" – movement is too erratic and you are as likely to shoot your teammate as to hit the opposing player. If you feel you must shoot into a melee, always aim slightly on the far side of the enemy, away from your teammate. Although this may make you slightly more likely to miss, it gives your teammate the best chance of surviving and just shooting close to the enemy player can disturb him and make him less likely to win the fight. If you have voice communication with your teammate in melee, tell him that you are aiming at the enemy he is fighting and tell him to back off. At this point you know he will move only backwards and defend, and you are safe to shoot directly at the opposing player.

Targets

An archer's primary targets are other archers. An archer protects teammates not just by killing other archers but by disrupting their fire, simply firing near them so they have to take cover or at least keep some awareness of you, can save a teammates life. Injuring enemy archers can mean your melee finish them off faster or that the archer has to stop firing to bandage.

Shooting an enemy melee player who is about to attack your teammate is fine. However shooting into melee should be attempted only when you are certain you will not injure your teammate.

Enemies in Travel Mode will be brought into the fall animation by an arrow hit and will be easy prey for any nearby melee or other ranged players, so where possible always shoot at a sprinting player. If you are aware of another ranged aiming at them it is tempting to hold your shot so that you get the kill shot on the fallen player; however the other ranged player is doing the same thing the sprinting opponent will safely get away.

Movement

If you are an archer, if you have just made a shot on an enemy player that may have alerted them to your position, move! Of course it is more difficult to aim while moving. Find cover and stay there while you charge your bow. Pop out only to shoot and return to cover for the next charge.

Field Awareness

When you have a tempting target, a downed player that you think may soon be revived, or a player about to bandage, it can be very easy to keep your bow drawn waiting for the perfect moment to shoot. No shot is worth dying for. Look around you between shots. If you have been still for a few seconds move and look around you even if it means losing an opportunity to shoot at that tempting target.

Try to position yourself so that your melee is between

you and any opponent. You will have more options for targets if you have the advantage of height; however this is also likely to make you more visible to opposing players.

Bows

Bows vary in their performance and so different bows are suitable for a different purpose. If a bow has a high arc you have to allow for the drop at the end of the arc and also for the longer time taken for the arrow to reach its target. However at the right distance you can use this to your advantage to reach opponents sheltering behind obstacles.

Generally speaking, bows with a flatter arc are more suitable for long range shots as the arrow will reach the target faster (less time for your target to move away) and you do not need to take distance into account in aim as much as for a higher arc. In game, bows with a higher arc can reshoot faster, so they are more suited to close range shots where the arc does not have such a great effect as it does on farther shots.

Throwing Weapons

The Champion and Warrior classes may select throwing weapons as their secondary weapon. To select a throwing weapon press MMB (middle mouse button). Hold MMB to aim the weapon and release MMB to throw the weapon. You can also select a throwing weapon by pressing the appropriate weapon number (default 2). Then you aim and throw the weapon by pressing and releasing the LMB. Throwing weapons do not regenerate but can be looted from the battlefield by running over them if you are not currently holding the maximum number for that weapon.

Aiming: When you select a throwing weapon, a crosshair appears on the screen to help you aim. You can cancel a throw, for axes only, by pressing RMB and you will return to your previous weapon. You can also parry an attack with a throwing axe.

Throwing weapons travel more slowly than arrows so you have to lead a moving target by a little more. They also drop much more quickly so their range is very limited.

Bouncing: Some terrain makes throwing weapons bounce. This can be used for hitting a player in the legs if he is hiding behind a shield. Walls and rocks also let you do bouncing throws. The damage is very low and even nil damage sometimes, but a hit can still serve as interruption of bandages or revives.

1v1 fights: If you engage in a 1v1 fight and feel uncertain you will win it, you will increase your chances if you manage to damage your opponent with your throwing weapons or make them drain their Stamina in order to dodge your throws. Then to make sure your opponent won't regain Stamina, keep an attack up so they will have to either block with shield or hold a parry up. While being forced to block or parry they regain Stamina at a slower rate.

Team Play: In a larger engagement the team that manages to score some hits with throwing weapons already has the upper hand. The best situation for this is when teams are on the smaller areas such as a bridge or narrow corridor/gateways.

Tip: You can interfere with a bandage either by dealing damage to your opponent or by raising your throwing-weapon towards your opponent as just the threat is likely to make him stop bandaging and instead flee or take an offensive posture.

If you find yourself outnumbered but your teammates are close by, one way of buying time is to charge a throw and keep aiming at your opponents without throwing.

Meanwhile, backpedal in the direction your support is most likely to come from. The risk of getting hit by your throwing-weapon will make most opponents raise their shields, and players without shields might start dodging and walking behind objects to avoid getting hit.

MOVEMENT & DODGING

On the battlefield, always keep moving. Unless you know for certain there is no enemy archer aiming at you, always assume there is and try to make them miss. Keep your movements erratic and unpredictable.

Dodging

Use the Alt key in combination with the movement keys (WASD) to dodge in any of the usual four directions (forward, back, left and right) but also the four in-between directions formed by holding both the keys for any two adjacent main directions (i.e. WA, AS, SD, DW). If you press Alt with no direction key the default direction is to dodge backwards.

Dodging uses quite a lot of Stamina but is useful to avoid being hit by melee or incoming projectiles. While in the dodging animation your character ducks slightly but enough to evade a blow (or a throwing weapon) aimed at the head. Be ready to dodge at all times while you are engaged in melee – that is often what you need to do to counter a special attack.

Be careful about dodging (especially in the default direction) when you are near fatal drops or water. As an archer it is good to develop the reflex to dodge whenever you are taken by surprise by an enemy sneaking up on you as it gives you enough time to draw your melee weapon.

Agile Fighter: This perk allows you to incorporate an attack at the end of the dodge manoeuvre. However, if you are in a duel and you know your opponent can parry it is not safe to use dodge attack as then when your opponent parries the attack you are stunned for long enough that he can hit you with a special attack, which will kill you.

If you dodge away as an opponent begins a swing at you, you can have time to move forward and strike with impunity at him before his swing animation ends and he can get another strike or a parry readied. Use the dodge attack when you think your opponents don't expect it.

Travel Mode

Travel Mode is entered by holding or tapping the left shift key in conjunction with the forward motion key (W); and exited by releasing or tapping the left shift key (or releasing the W key or pressing the backward motion, S key). While in Travel Mode you can *sprint*.

While in Travel Mode you can also run at an angle by holding the A or D key as well as W and Left Shift.

When you enter Travel Mode a quick animation puts away your weapon and when you exit Travel Mode another animation retrieves the weapon. You have to allow time for the animation before being able to fight, so do not end your sprint in strike range of an opposing player.

When you are in Travel Mode chasing an opponent you will gain a small speed boost so you are running faster than the chased player, soon you will be in range to tackle the fleeing player.

Tackling: When in vicinity of a sprinting opponent you will see a prompt to press E to tackle the opponent. A tackled player goes into a rolling animation and slowly regains their feet, if you are close enough this is plenty of time to kill them. For this reason sprinting is dangerous near to any foe. Any weapon hit, ranged or melee, will cause a sprinting player to fall into the "tackled" animation.

When you tackle a sprinting player your character gets a small speed boost in the direction of the falling player. When you reach the tackled player you should have plenty of time to aim your special attack to dispatch him. Be aware that if an opponent has the Chaser perk they will have an increased chase speed and be able to chase and tackle from a greater angle than normal. If a teammate tackles the same opponent and is between you and the opponent, your tackle can affect him instead of the intended target.

If you have the Juggernaut perk you cannot be tackled, or knocked down by a weapon hit, while you are sprinting.

While you are sprinting it is wise to be aware of whether there are any opponents near enough to tackle you, as this will be almost certain death. One way to look around you without losing momentum is to jump and turn while sprinting. This has the added benefit of helping to evade any arrows if an archer has you in their sights. One way to self-train the 180 degree jump while sprinting is to try it along the tree bridge in forest map as a misjump or any deviation in the intended direction will result in a fatal fall.

Jumping: When in Travel Mode you can jump further and higher than normal. This can help you to perform unusual manoeuvres on maps that may confuse your opponents. However if you use jump while moving from a high point to a lower point while in Travel Mode you may find the jump fatal even if you can safely drop off the high point when moving normally.

DAMAGE

Every player has a default Health amount of 100. You lose Health when hit by melee weapons or projectiles such as throwing weapons or arrows. The classes have different damage reductions:

The Warrior archetype has Medium Armour, with 30% damage reduction.

The Champion archetype has Heavy Armour, with 40% damage reduction.

The Skirmisher archetype has Light Armour, with 13% damage reduction.

Aim for the Head: Generally, if you want to be sure to deal a lot of damage, try to hit head or neck parts of opponents. Hitting the neck with a bladed weapon for 100 damage or more will decapitate the victim.

Mind your Perks: Keep an eye on your perks' descriptions as they can tell you how to deal more damage. The Skirmisher perk, for example, lets you deal 33% more damage with a headshot with a projectile.

Reflected Hits: Weapons that have hit something else first do reduced damage, if any.

Bandaging

When you take damage, make sure to take a look at your Health bar in the bottom of your screen. Any lost amount of Health can be regained by bandaging. The default button for bandage is B, which you have to stand still and hold for 6 seconds to complete bandaging. A complete bandage will give you full amount of hit points no matter how damaged you were.

When you need to bandage, try to find a safe spot not in view of enemies and in cover from projectiles. While you hold B to bandage you can move your mouse to change view. Make sure to look carefully around you while you bandage. While you bandage and move your view around to make sure you are safe, you can also use this time for tagging enemy players, using T for tag.

Teammates can bandage each other. This way the injured player reaches full Health more quickly (three seconds) than a self-bandage (six seconds), but two members of the team are stationary for the duration of the bandage. The bandage animation can be broken by either player moving but if the bandage is interrupted no Health will be regained.

Helping Teammates: You will soon see teammates in need of bandage. If you can, stay by them until they have finished their bandage because bandaging players often attracts enemies. If you have a shield you can cover teammates from projectiles while they bandage. In worst cases you can shield them with your body to make sure they are able to complete the bandage.

Tricking Enemies: You can use bandaging to trick enemy players. Act as if you need to bandage and turn your back to enemies. Start to bandage while you press B and turn your view so you can see your enemy's reaction. If they come close because they think you are unaware, press F to make a special attack. You can also use bandage to lure away players from bigger groups of enemies.

When you see an enemy bandage, remember that he might be trying to trick you into walking too close. If you have a throwing weapon or bow, use that on them. If you don't want to waste projectiles but still want to interrupt the bandage, walk towards them but try to zig-zag a bit if they attempt a special attack. If you walk towards them with raised weapon they are likely to think that you don't suspect anything and you can use this by making them do their special attack, and when they miss and try to recover, you can hit them with your own special attack.

Reviving

When someone has lost all their hit points (100) they will be laying on the ground in a state that is called knocked down. When you come across teammates who have been knocked down you can revive them by standing close to them pressing E for two seconds.

While you are moving towards knocked down teammates, make sure you don't have enemies around who can move in and catch you off guard while you revive. If you can use something as cover while reviving that is ideal as it will make you less of an obvious target.

If you have a shield you can lower the risk of getting hit by projectiles if you put the shield on your back and turn your back towards the direction your enemies are most likely to come from.

Request Aid: When knocked down you can press the left mouse button to request aid. Teammates will see a message that you are requesting aid and will know that you are knocked down. You should be aware of your surroundings and be sure that no melee is nearby and no opposing archer is covering your position before requesting aid.

Looting

When players die or drop any of their weapons, you will be able to pick them up by pressing Q. When you loot a weapon it will replace one of your weapons and your old weapon will be dropped for anyone else to loot.

You can loot any weapon or shield even if it is not available to your class in the profile editor, but you will drop any weapons/armour you no longer can equip because of the loot. You will always wield the weapon you picked up and replace the weapon you had wielded if your slots are full. Shields can be equipped only in a main weapon slot and will be wielded only if that slot also holds a one-handed weapon.

If you have thrown away any of the throwing weapons you had in any of your weapon slots, you will automatically pick up throwing weapons of that category by walking over them. If it is safe, move towards the direction you are aiming and throwing your weapons. This will make it easier for you to pick them up again if you miss your target.

If you have managed to kill someone who has thrown weapons in his body, you will be able to loot those when that player has respawned, because the body will then disappear.

MAKING THE MOST OF THE TUTORIAL

The basics of hitting and parrying can be learnt and practiced via the in game tutorial. After completing the melee practice you are able to pick up ranged weapons from the table for practice with the targets behind. The tutorial is reached via the main menu on entry to the game, or by navigating to the main menu with the Esc button once in game. This section will help you use the tutorial in the most effective way.

Melee

You can take the tutorial with either the sword or the one-handed axe just use the wield weapon keys 1 and 2 to switch between them. We recommended that you try it first with the sword and then with the one-handed axe.

When you are instructed to strike at the NPC (*Torsten the Tongueless*) use the "wrong" swing and you can keep going for as long as you like. You can also practice hits on the dummies at either side. Practice swinging at the different parts of his body and note the damage scores.

We recommend trying each swing many times before moving on to the next instruction. Try hitting high and notice the point at which the swing passes over the head. Also practice looking down as you swing and hitting low. Turn into your swing as you strike, lessening the time it takes the swing to connect.

Take this opportunity to notice the charge bar and the audio cue that accompanies it. After familiarising yourself with the charge bar try to time your attacks on full charge using just the audio cue. You can also use the dummies to explore how much the charge bar affects the damage numbers. The more you let the charge bar charge, the more damage is dealt.

Also note the Stamina bar, how it depletes with each attack, how fully charging your attacks gives the bar more time to refill and how repeated low charged attacks will quickly leave you with no Stamina. Listen for the Stamina audio cues and ensure you recognise them.

To learn the fastest way of hitting an opponent: stand facing a dummy and make a left swing, then stand with your left shoulder towards the dummy and make a left swing. When the weapon has less distance to travel it will hit much sooner but will do the same damage for the same charge. This principle holds true for all hits.

Ranged Weapons

Note that there are four targets, two within the walled area and two much further out on the hill. On the bench where you can select the throwing weapons. Note that there are an unlimited amount if you select them again after throwing. This let you try the different weapons and check how they drop depending on the distance you throw them.

Being familiar with how much the different throwing weapons drop is very useful when you move into playing against other players. Practice with each weapon until you can reliably hit at least the three closest targets. Remember these targets are not moving or fighting back and in game it will not be this easy. The dummies let you see how much damage is done by each of the different ranged weapons. Try hitting the dummies in the different parts of the body. Try moving as you throw to simulate throwing/shooting in combat where opponents are throwing back.

IMPROVING YOUR SKILLS

We look at what actually happens in game in melee and how you can get your first few kills and gain confidence. Then we look at what you can do to master the higher level skills.

First Steps to get a Kill in Melee

There are many elements and factors that make a player successful in this game. Some things will take months to learn even if you are able to practice for several hours per day. There are, however, some ways to quickly get into shape so that you can get kills. As you begin to get used to the game, it is important to find a comfort zone in the shape of a class/set of weapons.

Know your Weapon Length: No matter what weapon you start out with, you need to understand the length of it. This can be done by hitting an object (e.g. tree, stone, or wall). When you feel you have got the hang of where to stand in relation to your target to make hits connect, you can start to move around a bit in order to find out at what range your hits connect and at what range they miss.

Being sure of weapon length is very important because of the penalty you receive if you miss a swing. The miss penalty will make you unable to recover in time to parry a return swing or to quickly strike again yourself. So by knowing your range you can wait out your opponent and make him miss.

When you have practiced enough to understand the very basics of your reach and how to move in and out of reach you can already be of help to your team and even win some duels. However, when you are done hitting dead objects in order to get the hang of your weapon reach, you will notice that live opponents are harder to hit due to their movement.

Keep your Charge Up: When you are engaged in melee for the first time you will notice that because of how you and your opponent move, the reach and distances change all the time. It is important to remember to have an attack charged and, if necessary, to refresh the attack to make the charge bar full or close to full, when you choose to attack. The more charged the bar, the more damage you will deal.

Find a Duelling Partner: Your reach changes in relation to how you and your opponent move. This can be hard to master in a busy TDM (Team Death Match) or Conquest server. Find a TDM server that has the name Duel or 1on1/1v1. On this server you can fight against one other player without having to worry about anything else.

Players' skills differs considerably, and going up against veterans might not be helpful in the beginning. If you can find a player on a duel server who is close to your own skill level you can duel and practice together. You can even help each other out by deciding what to focus on. If both players want to get the hang of weapon reach, it is ideal to do it with another player who also needs to practice it.

Self-Tutoring

If you know the basic mechanics of the game and aim to improve and becoming better, you need to pay extra attention of especially one thing. Learn what makes you die or fail in certain situations. If you experience that you keep dying in the same way and similar situations this is the obvious hint of something you have to improve on and change.

To become good, it might help to have role models to take inspiration from, but if you want to become great you can't have any. If you have role models, their skill levels might become the limit for your progress. To become truly great, avoid anything that might act as obstacles for your continuous progress. (Having a social life does not count as an obstacle though!)

If you are a part of a clan or a competitive team, it is important that all its members know what kind of role they have in a match format. If you know you role you should focus on that role and spend your time fine tuning that. If you don't have regular training together with your clan/team, make sure to play with some of your clan mates every now and then to make sure you play well together.

Generally, even when you have gained a large amount of understanding and have thousands of hours effectively playing to keep improving at every aspect, it is important to keep stepping out of your comfort zone. You can play for years without improving a whole lot if you don't realize the importance of exploring all game play aspect of the game.

Feinting

Feinting is the method of getting past the opponent's parry by faking a swing from one direction and actually swinging from another direction. This is done by holding the LMB while moving the mouse for a strike, without releasing the LMB click the RMB to initiate a parry, this will interrupt your strike, as you click the RMB move the mouse in the direction of the next strike. This can be done repeatedly until the opponent misses the parry and you can strike. However you should watch for the opponent deciding to go on the offensive. A more advanced feint is achieved by releasing the LMB before clicking the RMB. This begins the strike and opponent will see the strike animation and hear the distinctive sound. The later into the strike you click the RMB, the more likely it is to deceive.

Buying Time

Your enemy is most likely to hesitate to approach and play offensively if you keep your melee weapon charged aiming at him. This gives you the initiative and, if needed, you can keep doing this until help arrives. Be aware of the possibility that your enemy dodge-attacks in your direction. If you do not wish to trade blows, you can dodge away to keep buying time. If you feel confident in your dodging abilities, you can dodge attack in the direction of your enemy and directly dodge back again to avoid trading blows. If you wish to repeat this over and over, make sure to keep a close check on your Stamina bar. The bar should be full if you decide to dodge-attack and dodge back, as this will ensure you have some Stamina left if something unexpected happens.

Fighting Outnumbered

If you get into a fight against two or more opponents and want to maintain control as much as possible, keep the attack charged and move around, facing first one enemy, then another. Keep doing this and they will be put in a defensive state and you will be able to dictate what happens next. With a charged attack you can strike towards the first opponent that decides to move towards you. Remember to observe what type of weapons you are dealing with, if your weapon is longer than theirs it will be a lot easier to control the initiative. It is also important here that you remember to keep moving and move in such a way that your enemies are forced to move where you want them to be so that you are able to know where they are at all times.

When you get more comfortable with the situation of fighting outnumbered, you can use several techniques to make being outnumbered an advantage for you. One way of doing this is to let your opponent think he has moved in on your back without you knowing. When he moves in to strike you, make sure to hit him first, preferably with a fully charged weapon. Or by letting your opponent think he has the jump on you, do a quick parry and strike back directly at him and if he is completely taken by surprise, you could keep attacking him and even get an easy kill from it. When you have some experience in being outnumbered and can keep calm in 1v2 or more, you can start to use being outnumbered to your advantage.

Another way of using being outnumbered to your advantage is to move yourself so you have player X in front of you and player Y opponent behind X Now while you fight player X just keep moving so that you always have him just in front of you, and make player Y unable to reach your flank. Imagine player X is the centre of a circle and you and player Y orbiting him, your aim is to maintain the position directly opposite player Y. While you block or parry player X, you charge your swing and check whether player Y tries to come in to support player X. You will then be able to hit at player Y. Y will most likely be unready to block or parry. This works even against experienced veterans.

Player Types

To win every confrontation you need to be able to tell what sort of play style your opponents have. Some examples:

The newbie: Some styles are obvious and easy to spot, like the new player who runs towards you for a very long time with his weapon charged. As the charge bar only stays charged for a very short moment, this player will deal little damage and the swing will also be slow. New players are easy to spot if they make their inexperience shown like this. Another sign of a new or inexperienced player is that he might try to use the special attack every time he thinks he is in range.

The Overconfident: Another player type is the overconfident or stubborn one. This can be a player who has played a lot but still keeps walking into fights he cannot win. A typical example is that this player walks into an open field with several archers positioned all over, making his life span very short as he try to cross the field. Since this type of player can be fairly competent in actual fighting you should be careful because he might not understand when he is beaten and will keep fighting to the end. Against this kind of player and similar types it is important to play patiently.

The Spammer: Another player type you have to play patiently against is the one who spams attacks as quickly as it is possible. Be careful not to meet spam with spam. Patiently block/parry and hit back, repeat over and over.

The Turtle is the kind of player who almost always moves with shield raised. The Turtle often backpedals as well while blocking with a shield, making fights against Turtles time consuming. If you keep hitting the shield it will eventually break, so try to maintain a high pressure and force the Turtle to block. When shield is gone it should be an easy kill.

The Kiter is often a type of player with a ranged weapon. The Kiter is often good at using the map design to make it hard to get to them. When you get close, they know how long they can wait until they have to change position. If you play melee and cannot catch up or do not have any throwing weapons, it is often better to leave this kind of player for your ranged teammates to deal with. Tag the Kiter and move on to the next target.

Keeping Track of Players

When you feel you have a general idea of how to play and move around without putting all energy into just navigating yourself around the map, you can hit tab to be able to see what pings players have and how many teammates and opponents you have to work with. Make this a habit and do it often, preferably once or twice per minute. This can help you make decisions on where to move and help you find enemies with very high pings. When you move around the maps, try to look around you 360 degrees as often as you can, to always have a general idea of where your teammates are and where the battles are happening.

Sounds: There are also plenty of sounds to listen for, to be able to tell where people are fighting and even what actions are made. Concentrate on sounds from parrying and special attacks. Make sure you have a high enough game volume to hear everything clearly – but not too high, to prevent any hearing loss.

"Mind like Water"

Much has been written about warfare and combat throughout history. Some manuscripts are thousands of years old. Between early writers as Sun Tzu and recent legend movie star fighter Bruce Lee there are many more or less well known writers and fighters. These writers have experienced combat first hand and have been fighting with death as a possible outcome.

Calm water is like a mirror and gives a picture of all that is around. Conversely troubled waters only reflect the turmoil within. When a person approaches a problem with calm and composure then like the reflection on calm water he sees everything. So also when a problem causes turmoil then like the troubled water on confusion is seen. Imagine an intellect as calm, a will as relentless and indomitable and a personality as adaptable as water and you will have envisioned a mind like water. (Sensei Takayuki Mikami)

While the "Mind like water" philosophy is helpful for the individual player it is of outmost importance for someone who leads and gives orders. If end up in a stressful situation where your team gets in trouble, people might start to talk with higher and stressed voices or even shout. Then if they know and trust their leader it is enough for him/her to talk calmly Objectively giving order and direct the team into what is needed for any given situation. A calm leader also gives his/her subjects the feeling that their leader is in control of the situation.

"Infect your Opponent"

For further on insights regarding the mind, I refer to the 17th century Japanese swordsman Miyamoto Musashi. In his *Book of Five Rings* he describes how we can infect our opponent with a mindset:

In single combat, you can win by relaxing your body and spirit and then, catching on the moment the enemy relaxes, attack strongly and quickly forestalling him. You can also infect the enemy with a bored, careless or weak spirit. You must study this well.

While a phrase like "you must study this well", might not seem very helpful it actually is, once you have given it some practice and time to reflect. The more I have come to learn and understood from playing War of the Roses and War of the Vikings, the more relevance and depth I have come to see in the text I quoted.

A way to make practical use of "infecting the enemy" is to start a fight with very slow and sluggish footwork and few attempts on hitting. The instant you see that your opponent has adapted and seems comfortable, make an extremely drastic change in your play. If you started very slow, suddenly be super-fast. If your opponent manages to adapt to that as well, try to slow down again. Stay in control of your opponent's rhythm.

This is something I often use and often see others use or fall for unconsciously. What often happens in a duel is that one player has a faster attack rhythm (generally called spamming) which makes the opponent unconsciously trying to match that rhythm. If a player is used to a very high pace where he relies on hitting all the time and rarely parries it is important that you recognize and acknowledge it. Don't fall into his phase trading blows and hope for the best. Instead, meet this fighting style – or any other extremely fast or extremely slow rhythm – with what is in your own comfort zone.

I find parrying the easiest way to deal with spam play styles. After a parry there is time to hit back. This way of dealing with spam might take some time and training to get comfortable with. But once you manage to, it is the safest way combined with sensible footwork.

CHAPTER 4: TEAM PLAY

This chapter introduces the concept of team play and helps you to understand how your play style affects others. We help you to identify key aspects to be aware of and how you can aid your teammates, bringing benefit to the team as a whole. *Ask not what your teammates can do for you but what you can do for your teammates!*

SQUAD BASICS

After team selection you are taken to the Squad Manager screen, or you can enter it at any time by pressing Esc and then Squad Selection. Click within a squad box to join a squad. The number of players allowed in a squad is a server setting. Players who have chosen not to be in a squad are called *lone wolves*.

The first person to enter a squad becomes the squad leader. He or she has the option to:

- Click the animal icon to select the animal after which the squad will be named.
- Kick players from the squad.
- Click the Lock icon to toggle squad Lock/Unlock. Other players cannot enter a locked squad.

SQUAD PLAY

In every game mode it is very helpful for you and your team if you join a squad as soon as the game starts. It often happens that the team with most players in squads is the most successful. This could be because the more experienced players know how to join, and benefit from being part of, squads. But even if a team is stacked with veterans who are lone wolves they might get overwhelmed and beaten by newer players who do use squads.

Squad Spawning

In Team Death Match (TDM) the spawn system will prioritize spawning a squad member near other members of the squad, which spawns them in in a useful location but also gives protection of numbers. However Lone Wolves often spawn one at a time with risk of having to deal with a large portion of the enemy team.

Squad mates are outlined in green. You can see the health bar of squad mates and can therefore make appropriate decisions about helping them to bandage. The squad leader has an icon before his name tag visible only to squad mates.

Tagging

When in a squad you can tag an enemy by pressing T while keeping the cursor over him. The tagged enemy will be highlighted red for all members of your squad. Tagged enemies can be seen even behind obstacles, so it is clear to you when they are trying to bandage, hide or sneak up on teammates.

Tagging is one of the biggest strengths of a squad. Each squad member can tag one enemy player, and should do so. You can also use being tagged to your advantage. If you

fake being hurt and desperate for bandage you can often lure one or a few opponents to chase you. If you know where your teammates are you can lure the opponents to your teammates to get some easy kills and score for your team.

TEAM TACTICS

It is important to be observant of when you can strike the opponents who are busy fighting your teammates. In fact, be more aware of this than of when you can damage the opponent who currently fights you. If you play like this together with one teammate against two enemies (2v2), and your teammate also plays like this, it will make your opponents confused as they don't know from where and from whom the attacks will come.

Don't Hit your Friends!

When you engage enemies together with teammates, make sure to use attack directions relevant to your teammate's position. Otherwise you risk hitting teammates. For example, if you have a teammate on your left you should use either an overhead attack or a right swing.

Server-settings might vary but if friendly fire is on you risk hurting your teammates. Even if settings allow you to hit teammates without penalty, it is still not without risks to do so. If you hit your teammate while he tries to parry an incoming attack he will lose the parry and is likely to get hit by the opponent. When you fight alongside teammates be very careful to not walk into teammates' weapon swings. If space allows it, try to engage enemies with some distance from teammates.

Helping Teammates in Trouble

Often you will see teammates in trouble, getting hit by arrows or melee weapons. When this happens you can *a)* make the archer busy and hope your teammate will manage on his own in the melee fight, or *b)* engage in the melee fight as well.

If you are comfortable with parrying, I would advise you to get in front of your teammate and make yourself the target. This gives your teammate the option to step back and bandage. But be aware of that even if you have drawn enemies to fight you instead of your hurt teammate, one or a few might try to run past you to kill of your bandaging friend.

Two Against One

When you and a teammate come across one enemy (2v1) and this enemy seems confident in parrying all your attacks, you have two options:

CHAPTER 4: TEAM PLAY

- While your teammate is trading blows, try to get into position to make a special attack.
- A more efficient method is something called chain of attacks. Hold your attack charged (refresh the swing whenever your charge bar depletes) and be ready to hit the enemy the moment he changes his block to protect himself from your teammate. You can do this over and over, and your enemy will have to choose which attack he gets hit by.

Support from Archers

When you play melee and you have archers behind you, try to move in a way that gives your archers clear shots. On smaller bridges or other tight spots you can choose either the left or right side to make evasive manoeuvres to avoid getting hit by enemy archers. This will give your team's archers an area to shoot through without risking hitting you.

While you are engaged in a melee fight with an opponent and have archer teammates covering you, try to move your opponent around in order to make him an easy target for your team's archers. This is also how you can make opponents turn their back on your melee teammates. This lets them come in from behind and possibly deal massive damage.

Breaking a Stalemate

On some maps you will notice how narrow and bottlenecked parts of a map might create a state of stagnation where neither team is able to push through and gain the upper hand. When this happens, there are two quite drastic ways of breaking the stalemate:

Try to push through the lines from the front and position yourself behind the line of enemies. This will likely make some of them turn around in attempts to hit you.

While they do this your own team should be able to deal some serious damage to them, making it possible to further push through and break their lines completely. This puts you at high risk but might also result in high reward for your team.

If you know the map well you can run around to appear behind the enemy line you can hit enemies in the back – either opponents who are standing back to shot or those that wish to step back to bandage. Sometimes it is enough to just show up behind the enemy line without attacking. Your presence will make the enemy team focus on you, making the pressure on your team less.

Use the Terrain

Make sure your team finds and makes use of defensive positions on the battlefield. It can be an area which only has one or few small entrances. In a place like this the archers can stand calmly and take their time to aim and shoot, and melee players have a safe place to fall back to for bandage.

In open spaces it is important to push and pull the enemy team around to suit your current needs. If you fight your enemies while they keep their archers back to shoot at you, try to move the melee battle closer towards the archers. Keep the enemy melee players between you and the enemy archers as you keep pushing towards the archers. This forces the enemy archers to either move away to find a safer spot or shift to their melee weapon and support the melee fighters.

CHAPTER 5: GAME MODES

This chapter introduces the different game modes and explains the aim of each. Understanding the goals of each game mode and its victory conditions will give you the edge in vanquishing the opposition.

TEAM DEATH MATCH (TDM)

TDM is a game mode with the two teams Vikings and Saxons simply killing each other. The opposing team will have red names and you must kill as many of them as possible while not being killed yourself.

If you are killed you will respawn and start again until the round timer reaches the set time or one team reaches the set number of kills for a win.

You may enter a TDM map at any point in the round. Usually the teams will be balanced. If there are equal numbers on each team you may join either but if one team has X fewer players you will have to join that team (where X is Player Threshold set in server settings). The length of the round (Time Limit) is a server setting.

Victory Conditions

- Accumulate a number of points, Win Score, set in the server settings (often set as 100).
- Have the most points at the Time Limit set in the server settings.

Accumulating Points

Team points are added only when an opposite team member is a confirmed kill – that is when they are not revivable (i.e. instakilled, executed or suicides). When an opposing player is knocked down but can still be revived, the kill is added to your personal score, but not to the team score. When a knocked down player is executed this is not counted as a kill on your personal score.

Maps for TDM

Cliff
Docks
Forest
Icefloe
Stronghold
Tide

Tactics for TDM

- Watch your Health (the blood splatter around the edges of your screen). Always try to bandage after taking damage Archers and players with throwing weapons will be on the lookout for bandaging players, find a safe place where you are likely to be unseen and undisturbed for six seconds.
- Try to stay near a teammate and work together. In particular, melee players should guard their archers. Archers

often watch a knocked down player as a reviver is an easy kill. If your teammate was killed by an archer, be sure the archer is otherwise occupied before reviving.

- There is no point in reviving someone if he will take 50 damage while getting up (which takes six seconds), so be prepared to protect the victim with a shield or parry.
- Archers often have tunnel vision and sneaking up on them from behind is relatively easy. In TDM in particular, enemies often seem to forget you are there if you are out of sight for a few seconds.

CONQUEST (CQ)

Conquest is a game mode which all about capturing Objectives. Kills and deaths are of no significance, and in fact sometimes dying rather than killing is of advantage to your team. The skill in this mode is in recognising when to push for the next Objective point and when to hold. Killing the enemy between the objective points is often a disadvantage to your team. So the team with the best teamwork and players who understand the mode is most likely to win.

At the start of the round each team spawns at one or two (map dependent) spawn points at either end of the map. There will be four or five Objective points (map dependent) at the start of the round. The middle Objective (if there is one) will be neutral and the other four points will be owned by the team that spawns nearby. Objective points have a beam of light projecting into the sky to make them easy to locate.

You may enter a Conquest map at any point in the round. Usually the teams will be balanced – if there are equal numbers on each team you may join either, but if one team has a fewer players you will have to join that team. After death you can respawn. A team will spawn near the Objective that it holds that is farthest from the original spawn point.

The respawn timer is a server setting and can be Pulse or Personal. In either case the time is also a server setting.

Pulse: The respawn timer constantly ticks down and all dead players will respawn when it hits zero.

Personal: Your respawn timer starts when you die and you will respawn it reaches zero.

Victory Conditions

- Take all the Objective points.
- Hold the most Objective points at the Time Limit (set in server settings).
- If the teams hold the same number of Objective points the round is a draw.

Objective Points

Each map has four or five Objective points. Each point is indicated by a short pillar or circle on the ground with a round icon above it. The icon indicates the current ownership of the point, with a Mjolnir (Vikings) or Cross (Saxons) and a colour. Blue means your team and red means the enemy team. These icons are also listed at the top of the screen underneath the timer, for a quick indicator of the current status of the round.

Capturing an Objective: When a player steps inside the capture range of an Objective point to be captured, four things happen:

- There is a chiming audible cue and the bar below the icon will gradually fill with blue.
- The appropriate indicator at the top of the screen will have

a yellow outline and flash between the current state and the "in contention" grey with crossed yellow swords symbol.

- A message indicating the point is being captured will flash across all players' screens.
- The icon for the previous capture point for the capturing team will have a lock and chain added indicating that it is no longer available to be captured.

If the point is not fully captured but no player remains within the capture range, the bar will gradually revert to its original state. If the point is fully captured, this happens:

- An audible cue sounds.
- A message is lashed across the screen for all players.
- The appropriate icons change colour.
- The next Objective point for the attacking team has the lock and chain icon and a timer counting down from 25, when the timer reaches 0 the lock and chain disappear and the point is available for capture.

Capturing Objective Points

If one team has a player in the capture zone, the Objective point starts to shift in the direction of that team as long as no opposing player is in the capture zone. It takes a single unopposed player 20 seconds to capture a neutral Objective. It will take two unopposed players about three seconds less. For each extra player standing in the capture zone the increment by which the capture time is decreased is slightly diminished. So the speed of transition is slightly faster if the capturing team has more members at the Objective point. However the Objective's ownership will not switch if the other team has a live player in the capture zone. If one team already owns the Objective point, the opposing side has to neutralize it before it can start to take ownership.

Maps for Conquest

Cliff
Docks
Forest
Ravine
Stronghold

Tactics for Conquest

It is always an advantage for a team going forward to leave one player at the last Objective point to prevent a member of the opposing team capturing it while the rest of the team goes forward. One player is enough as other defending players should respawn in the area.

- As kills do not count towards the team winning the round, avoiding the opposing players except at the Objective points is recommended.
- When your team is moving forward it is of no benefit to kill opposing players (unless they are standing in the capture area) as they will respawn close to the Objective point your team is trying to capture.
- Consider taking the Juggernaut perk as there is a lot of running between Objective points.
- Fighting inside the capture zone whilst keeping your opponent outside helps to capture Objective points.
- Archers should try to stand in the capture area and shoot out. Where possible, melee should prevent opposing players reaching archers in the capture zone.
- A team on the defensive should try to have every player in the capture zone.

ARENA AND PITCHED BATTLE

Arena is the much smaller version of Pitched Battle. PB is a single life game mode where if you die you will wait until the next round to respawn. PB is the most competitive game mode and Arena the most intense and fast paced version. PB is the mode used for competitions and attracts the most skilled players of the game. Teamwork is useful in the other game modes but essential in PB.

Usually the teams will be balanced – if there are equal numbers on each team you may join either but if one team has X fewer players you will have to join that team (where X is Player Threshold set in the server settings).

A round will not start until there are enough players. This number is set as Minimum Players per Team in server settings. Teams spawn at either end of the map. The spawn points swap between each round.

After death you cannot respawn until the beginning of the next round. While dead you may watch the progress of the game from the viewpoint of any live player unless the camera is locked (a server setting used for competitive matches). While dead your text chat will be prefixed with "dead" and will be visible only to other players whose characters are dead.

When the timer comes close to ending (round duration is a server setting) the playable area will shrink around a central point, to bring players into close proximity.

Victory Conditions

Each battle consists of several rounds (the number of rounds is a server setting) on one map until one team reaches the Win Score server setting. Your team wins a round if:

- You kill everyone on the enemy team.
- Every member of the opposing team yields or leaves.

Maps for Arena

Cliff

Crag

Docks

Gauntlet

Icefloe

Monastery

Ruins

Sanctuary

Stronghold

Tide

Maps for Pitched Battle

Cliff

Docks

Forest

Ravine

Stronghold

Strategies for Arena / Pitched Battle

- Health and armour are more important in this game type. Consider having perks for these.
- Revive your teammates whenever it is safe to do so.
- Guard teammates while they are being revived. 50 damage will permanently kill them while they are in the animation for revival (six seconds).
- Stop enemy melee fighters from reaching your archers.
- If you are a good shot with throwing weapons, injuring your opponents at the start of the round can decide the battle (especially on the small maps).
- If you are a less good shot with throwing weapons, save them to finish off injured players looking for a safe place to bandage.

- Stay within easy reach of teammates, try to outnumber opponents.
- Get into squads and tag archers, and any opponent who might need a quiet place to bandage.
- Archers on the flanks can prevent opponents from finding a safe place to bandage.
- If archers are preventing bandaging, teammates can help by covering the bandaging player with their shield (or body if necessary).
- Pressuring archers should be a priority whenever possible.
- A player who is revived will not count as alive until the six-second revival time is up, therefore a round can be won if the last alive player on a team is killed while his teammate is in the reviving animation.

DUEL

While there is not yet an actual duel game mode, some servers are labelled as duel servers. These have strict rules to facilitate two players fighting in a 1 v 1 style. Duel servers are very useful to practice with each weapon without having to worry about field awareness and fighting multiple opponents. A new player will often find duel servers a good place to learn the basics and ask questions.

Duelling Server Etiquette

- To initiate a duel, challenge a player by raising an upward parry in their direction while in front of them.
- To accept a challenge, return the upward parry.
- A duel is not started until a challenge is accepted.
- Do not attack any player unless the challenge has been made and accepted.
- Keep your distance from duelling players.

- If you win the duel, bowing before the defeated is a sign of respect.
- If you are observing a duel, you can crouch to indicate you are not available to duel.
- Some servers will have a "no archers" rule as archery can interfere with melee duels.
- "Randoming" – hitting a player who has not accepted a duel – may result in a ban from the server.
- If you wish to limit the options available in a duel (e.g. no throwing weapons) make this clear before starting the duel.
- Many players will admit defeat by stopping to bandage. The polite response is to wait for them to finish (or take the opportunity bandage yourself if necessary).
- On official duel servers, if someone who is unaware of the duel rules enters a duel server, the correct response is to inform them politely that it is a duel server and has rules.

CHAPTER 6: THE BATTLEGROUNDS

This chapter gives a brief introduction to all eleven map levels available in the game. We indicate the main areas, helping you to locate the key strategic points on each level.

General Notes

- Water is a boundary and will kill. Depth of death varies but is generally at standing height.
- Many fences have gaps through which it is possible to shoot.
- Most maps have places from which you can safely jump. But remember a jump has a small stun on landing, giving a player following you a free hit.
- When you are dead it is possible for you to see the character in your profile selection screen on the specific part of the map shown in that screen.

CLIFF

This is a long, large map leading from a monastery high on a cliff, though a village, down a cliff path to the beach below. The map is quite dark as a storm is in progress, the

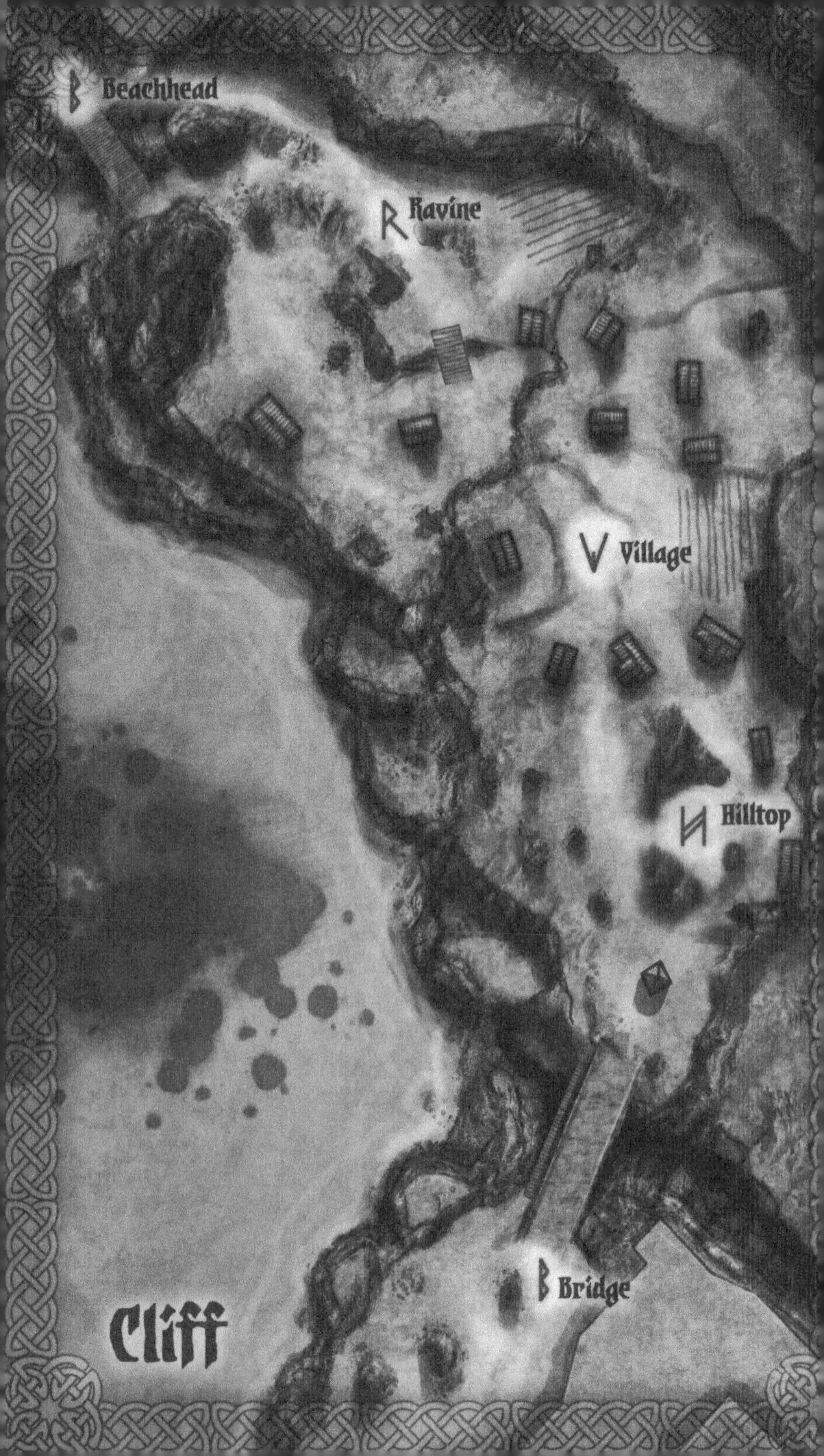

ᛒ Beachhead
ᚱ Ravine
ᚡ Village
ᚺ Hilltop
ᛒ Bridge
Cliff

gloomy sky being occasionally lit by lightening. Ambient sounds include the monastery bells, cawing crows, the moaning wind and thunder, and down at the beach the waves lapping at the shore.

Outside the unjumpable monastery wall is a level clifftop area bounded by a sheer drop. This is the Saxon spawn for Conquest matches. A doorway and passage breach the wall and provide some cover, but being caught in here is a death trap and is best avoided. From all of the clifftop, but even from the extreme end by St Hilda's grave, it is possible for an archer to hit targets at the cliff path and even on the beach. The clifftop has a few large boulders providing cover. The only entrance/exit from this area is the stone bridge across the gorge.

The wide bridge rises slightly in the middle giving a little cover at either end, as archers routinely target the areas around the ends of the bridge make the most of what cover there is. The seaward side of the bridge has a lower makeshift walkway reached by a bridge side path at either end. It is possible to jump down to the walkway from lower ends of the bridge, but jumping from the middle section is fatal. It is possible to shoot down to the walkway. However the side passages on the walkway provide cover from archers above, and to some extent from those at the ends of the path. The bridge has wooden projections on either side, it is possible to jump onto these, from above or from each other, however it is very dangerous and has no use.

Beyond the bridge is a rocky height, with the Hilltop Objective. Hilltop is overlooked by a raised cottage garden, which provides cover and line of sight for protecting Hilltop. Below the hill on the seaward side is the shell of a house set amongst boulders. These provide cover and line of sight over Clifftop, the bridge and the lower path.

Hilltop is difficult to attack from the village and a coordinated attack using the right and left flanks in addition to the middle path is most likely to succeed.

The village is large and dominated in the centre by a huge cross. The Village Objective point is adjacent to the cross, partially shielded on three sides by a low rock wall topped with a fence. This wall provides cover for defenders wanting to bandage but also for attackers sneaking up to the Objective point. On the land side of Village is a fenced orchard with only three gateways, the furthest one leading on to the heights on the landward end of the Village, from where a ladder leads down to the cliff path. From the heights archers have line of sight over the Ravine Objective point, the top of the cliff path and the seaward side of the village. On the seaward side of the village a rocky outcrop shields a lower path, with a plank bridge across a small (and jumpable) gorge. That is useful for sneaking up behind Village defenders. On the beach side of the plank bridge it is possible to jump up on the rocky outcrop as another sneaky approach to Village Objective point.

Near the top of the path leading from the village to the Beachhead Objective point is the Ravine Objective point. From the village three paths lead to the Ravine, one from the wide plank bridge and from the cliff side of the Village approaching from either side of an unclimbable rocky hill. Between the two cliff side paths a rocky ledge gives cover and line of sight for attacking the Ravine but is vulnerable to defenders spawning close by.

A wide Beach Path marked by stout, tall poles leads to a covered, wooden bridge and the Beachhead Objective point. From Ravine there are three paths sloping to meet the beach path. From the top of the beach path a hidden right fork takes you along a lower path that hugs the other edge of the ravine and leads under the bridge to come up behind the Beachhead Objective point. It is possible to jump from the Beachhead area on to the lower path. In particular jumping from the left side of the covered bridge is a fast shortcut. It is possible to jump from the Ravine end of the bridge (or any other part of the bridge) onto the tree growing in the ravine. It is possible to jump from the bridge to the fenced off cliff side and walk around the cliff.

Arena Fights in Cliff

For Arena mode only a small section of the TDM Cliff map is used, this is the Clifftop area. The spawns are at the monastery side of the Bridge and at the cliff side of the monastery wall. Many of the boulders are low enough to shoot over but high enough to give good cover, exposing only the head.

The bridge spawn has three large boulders providing some cover. A short distance along the bridge, are the out of bounds markings and crossing these will give you the message to return to the battle within five seconds. The lower bridge path provides some cover and the out of bounds message appears at the end of the first arch.

The monastery spawn has one large boulder providing cover above head height, from this a low wall runs along the cliff top towards the bridge, terminating just before the slope to the lower bridge path. The monastery spawn is backed by large flat rocks, above head height, which slope slightly back. The out of bounds markings are at the back of these rocks, cutting off the corner with the tree and grave which are accessible on TDM and Conquest. The slope of the rocks provides a little cover for anyone that jumps up there and it is possible to jump down behind the rocks and back up within the five seconds allowed when out of bounds. Using ranged weapons from these rock tops and attacking opposing players as they jump up can give an advantage although you are exposed to enemy archers.

There is a large above head height boulder in the middle of the area, teams will gain an advantage if they push forward together and hold the rock from which they can cover all other areas of the map apart from the Doorway and the lower path. The Doorway into the monastery provides some cover from distant archers, but is a disadvantage if a ranged enemy approaches the entrance.

CRAG

A very small map set in a cliff side. A squashed ellipse shape with one long edge bounded by a sheer rising cliff (wall) and the other by a sheer drop (cliff). Ambient sounds include wind whistling, rocks tumbling, and bird calls. The spawn points are at each small end of the ellipse.

On the cliff side the ground is slightly lower. An upper path which runs along the wall is high in the middle and slopes down at each end. In roughly the middle of the map is a cromlech with a tall upright stone at the cliff side and a capstone sloping down from the top of the upright to the upper path. You can walk onto the lower end of the capstone from the upper path. Fighting on the capstone gives the advantage of fighting on a slope, which disconcerts many melee, and the choice to jump down if hard pressed on the stone or in order to help a teammate below. It is possible to safely jump from the higher end of the stone but care must be taken not to fall of the cliff. If you are confident at this it is very dangerous for opponents to directly follow you. An overhead attack made while under the capstone will in some places hit the stone and is best avoided.

The right hand spawn is slightly nearer the cromlech giving this spawn the advantage in taking the only feature

Crag

Spawn

Spawn

of the map (cromlech). This spawn has a couple of high boulders flanking the wall that are climbable and make a good shooting spot.

The left hand spawn has a sloping rock alongside the wall which slopes upwards away from the upper path and makes a small, defensible archer spot. A team would not want many archers on this map as it is so small there is little space to be out of melee in time to draw a bow.

DOCKS

A large map in a U-shape around an island. At certain points you can hear ducks and near the ford you can hear frogs. Other ambient sounds include lapping water, rustling leaves, crackling flames and bird calls.

The highest point of the map has a Longhouse (If you aim a bow through the door of the Longhouse you can see the interior). On the island side the ground slopes down and has a small drop to a board walk above the inlet, which proves a second, hidden approach to the Longhouse area.

You can enter the small A-shaped building near the lower part of the Longhouse, this is a good place to bandage but a bad place to be trapped. The Conquest Objective point called longhouse is located below the longhouse between two walls, with boulders interrupting the open ends. This is a very defensible spot if melee players hold the forward rocks while archers hold the high ground.

The Longhouse Objective point has only one natural attacking route, from the open end facing the walkway and archers on the Objective are well placed in good cover to protect that route. However archers often place themselves on the high ground above the Objective, where they are a good target for any opposing ranged lower down the hill or who have flanked them from the boardwalk.

Docks

Riverbank

Storehouse

Tavern

Longhouse

From the Longhouse the ground slopes down past some Beach Huts. On the inlet side a lower boardwalk has two ladders up to the main area. If the ladders are covered by archers they are dangerous to climb, but if they are not overlooked they are useful to get behind those defending the Longhouse Objective point area.

Some of the huts have paths around the back, allowing sneaky approaches to opponents. One has a gap underneath through which it is possible to shoot an unwary opponent. From the lower boardwalk there is a crossing to the island through shallow water, known as Frog Ford.

Below the beach huts is a tavern with a square garden. From the garden a wooden bridge leads to the island and further on a gateway leads to a wooden storage platform, either end of this platform is blocked by a breakable obstruction at the start of the map. The Tavern Objective point is between the tavern and the bridge. Defenders have to watch approaches from the bridge, the lower boardwalk, the main path from the longhouse, the back of the Tavern and the gateway to the storage area.

The bridge is a choke point, which is possible for a few players to defend. If the bridge is competently held attackers have the option of going around either by Frog Ford or through the wooden storage area. From the island end of the bridge it is also possible to flank defenders by jumping on some pilings and then to the boardwalk (or the wall).

The bridge has a support on either side, which is possible to climb and has a vantage point over much of the map. However, anyone standing here is also an excellent target for archers from many points on the map.

The wooden platform starts the game with its two entrances blocked by breakable obstruction. This area has a lower and an upper level with a hanging platform onto which you can jump. The upper level has line of sight to

Riverbank Objective point and to the garden above the Tavern Objective point. In TDM players can spawn in the blocked off wooden platform area. They can exit without breaking the barriers by jumping from the high platform on the Riverbank side.

The island has plenty of cover and from here it is possible to shoot at most other areas of the map and also to cover the three choke points. A small tent shaped building, near the wooden bridge, is good cover for bandaging. The large stone forge building at the end of the bridge has a raised, external area overlooking the bridge and Frog Ford.

Between the forge, the tent hut and the wooden bridge in a dip in the path is the Storehouse Objective point. This can be approached from all sides but is shielded from long range arches by its lower level and the buildings.

From Frog Ford you can walk on the river side rocks below the forge to within about a yard of the bridge, where you inexplicably fall down dead. This can be a good place to bandage as it is not much used. Just above this, a narrow path runs below the forge, between the ford entrance and the wooden bridge path, allowing an unseen approach to the head of the bridge or the Objective point.

From the Island a stone bridge leads to a low lying fish drying area, known as Riverbank. Here the Objective point is slightly shielded by fencing and boulders. A wooden pier (and boulder outcrop) leads to a boat, this is a good shooting spot but a bad place to be cornered. The stone bridge also has a path underneath it, which is useful to get across the water while evading archers.

Docks in Arena Fights

The Docks Arena map is a small segment of the larger TDM map, consisting only of the island. Both bridges are removed and the out of bounds line is at the bottom of the slope to Frog Ford, which is blocked off by boulders and a fence. One spawn is upslope on the path from the ship, "Ship Spawn"; the other is by the well above Frog Ford, "Frog Spawn".

Ship spawn gives the option of taking cover downslope to the right or left and trying to flank the opposition from the cover the lower ground level affords. To the left, the path around the forge has a narrow lower path which is accessible from both sides, so two opponents may meet with no room to dodge and the first to use their special usually lives. There is a higher path accessible only from the Ship Spawn side giving the advantage of height and allowing ranged to attack with no fear of a direct melee response. To the right, the lower path of Pier Walk slopes up at the gap between the two buildings. The very narrow path around the second building echoes the narrow path around the Forge.

Frog Spawn has the option of taking cover behind the two large buildings, flanking either side or going through the middle. Frog spawn is at a disadvantage when flanking to the right due to the inaccessible high area at the forge.

FOREST

A large map in an L shape. The boundaries are a river on one side and steep cliffs on the other. Ambient sounds include rustling leaves, trickling water, falling rocks, birds, howling and distant horns. The map is quite open with several paths to each area. However there are some dead ends in which it is wise to avoid being trapped.

The lowest end of the map is a pier with a Viking boat and a camp with tents. The Conquest Objective, called Landing, is located in this camp. In Conquest, Vikings spawn at this end of the map.

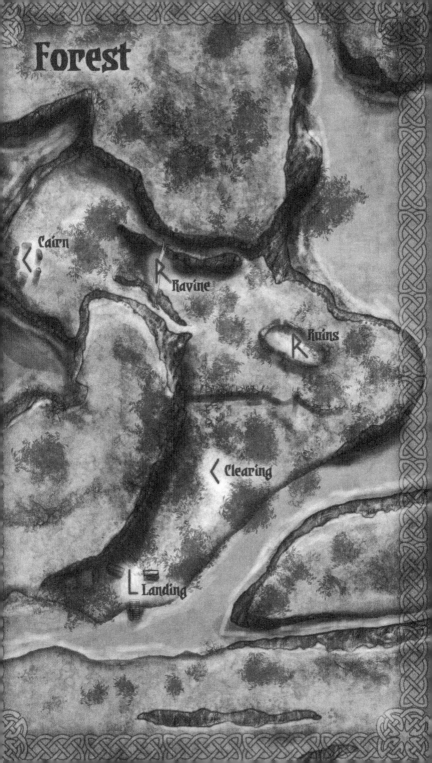

Forest

Cairn

Ravine

Ruins

Clearing

Landing

There is plenty of cover at camp, and changes of level, affording opportunities both to shoot from cover and to sneak up behind archers and engaged melee. From the pier the map is bounded by a shoreline on the right and the ground slopes upwards to be bounded by a cliff on the left.

The Conquest Objective point, called Clearing, is located towards the cliff side, with very little cover. In this glade cover is provided by rocks and trees. However the high ridge before the ruins provides good archer spots as the does the rise at camp. When in the glade one should always be aware of the possibility of archers with good view and the advantage of height on three sides. Beyond the glade there is a change of level with a wall on the higher side, with several paths up to an area of ruins. The river makes 90 degree turn here and bounds this area on two sides.

Falling off the cliff into the river is fatal. The central path slopes up through a double arch set into the wall. On the left a path slopes steeply up beyond the end of the wall, this path is a spur from the arch path or can be reached from below by a ladder. On the right a grassy path slopes gently up the rock to the far edge of the wall, the area at the top here has a good view of the glade and makes a good archer spot. The wall is climbable on the river side of the archway, and where it is part of the ruins of a round tower. The Conquest Objective point is at the large cross inside the ruined church. It can be approached from all sides and the ruined walls provide cover on higher ground for archers shooting into the church. Many ruin walls are climbable and make good archer spots, especially if a friendly melee fighter prevents opponents from getting to the archer.

A narrow valley with a high path on either side is bridged by a fallen tree. In TDM the high paths are favoured over the valley as they afford a better view for and of archers. Falling or jumping from the high paths in some places ends in death but in some place can be safely achieved; an awareness of the safe spots can save your life (and kill an opponent if they follow you in a jump). For this reason though the valley is rarely watched and can be a safer route between the henge and the ruins. In Conquest, the Ravine Objective point is located in this valley making it difficult to defend.

The tree bridge is an unsafe place as lateral movement will end in a fall and death, so avoidance is not possible. If two melee fighters are on the bridge the first to get in a special is likely to kill the other.

The valley opens out in to a sloping area bounded by cliffs falling to the river. The main feature is a partly fallen stone henge. On the right is a beautiful waterfall. The high paths from the Ravine have good line of sight over the henge, and are therefore useful archer spots.

On the left as the valley opens to the henge is a fence behind which is a slightly lower lying area, which is often overlooked and therefore is a good place to bandage. On the right as the valley opens to the henge is a raised area with a large rune stone, giving archers good line of sight over the henge and useful cover.

Forest in Arena Fights (Ruins)

This is a small segment of the Forest map which includes the church area. The area is bounded by water at a higher level than in Forest. The spawns are at either end of the church on the long axis. The church area is at a lower level and so archers should remain on the higher ground outside, but the walls provide cover for melee to reach archers. The abundant cover and the change in level will prompt most organised teams to move either left or right at spawn

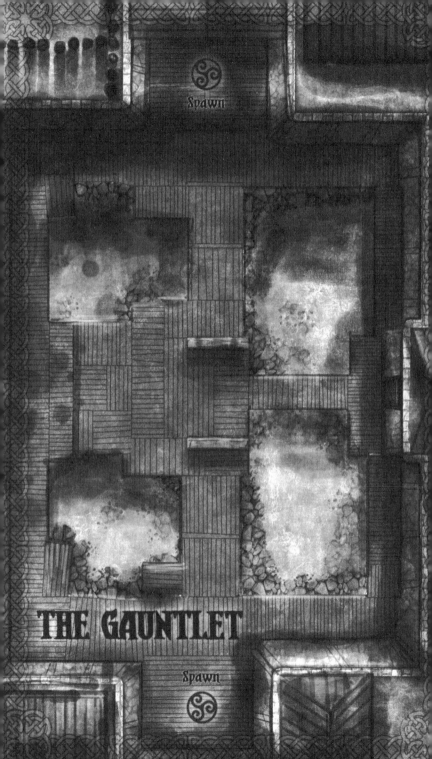

Spawn

THE GAUNTLET

Spawn

and avoid the central lower ground, but care has to be taken not to move too close to the water as in a melee fight. Using the central area as a quick crossing to sneak up on unaware opponents is a valid but risky tactic.

GAUNTLET

A small, square open map with raised wooden areas above a mire. All parts are walkable. Ambient sounds include lapping water, creaking wood, banging. On one side there is a raised platform (stage) midway between the spawn points. On the stage three pillars provide a little cover. Teams spawn in an opening set out of the square at the top and bottom edges.

Boardwalks run all around the square. The boards are just a visual delineation as there is no movement boundary between the boards and the mire except at the stage wall, where a jump is required to get on or off the boardwalk.

Set into the wall opposite the stage is set a narrow stone "lip", jumping onto it gives a slight height advantage. The doorway opposite the stage protrudes just enough to give an archer on the lip cover from archers at the opposing spawn.

In the centre, in a line between the two spawns, are two short wooden fences. These fences provide cover from the archers who remain at the spawn, and protection from a frontal attack. However, there are gaps in the boards though which it is possible to shoot. Reaching the second fence after spawn gives an advantage as it gives the first fence to fall back to if necessary.

ICEFLOE

A small, slightly oval shaped map based on an ice floe, with a small island in the seaward side. Ambient sounds include whistling winds, the ice creaking and breaking

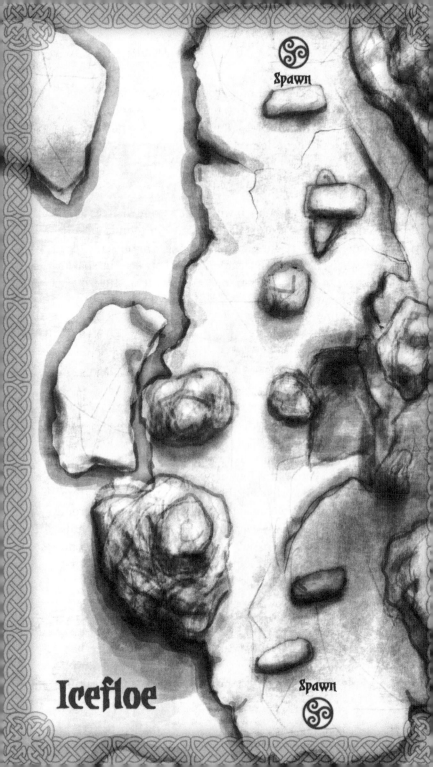

Spawn

Spawn

Icefloe

and when you are near a cliff edge, clumps of snow falling. The map is bounded by ice cliffs on one long side and the sea on another. The spawns are at either end of the oval, on the top or bottom of the map.

The main features on the map are large boulders which provide cover. Each spawn has a large boulder in front of it. There is an upper path running along the cliff edge. This has a lower ledge before an unjumpable chasm.

A large Ice island on the seaward side is partially hidden by the huge boulders. It takes about the same time to run from either spawn to the island. The island can only be reached by jumping on to it. The island can be covered by archers on the right spawn side but not the left.

MONASTERY

A medium sized, rectangular map based on a cloister. Ambient sounds include monastery bells, breaking waves, seagulls, crackling flames when near torches and distant shouts when you are near to the arcade wall.

One long edge is bounded by the wall arcade running along a wall, with tall buildings at each end. This arcade continues along the long edge of the buildings and ends just before the sea wall. It provides enough cover for bandaging and to move mostly unseen.

The other long edge has an open arcade, the further side having a fatal drop to boulders below. It is possible to jump from the upper part of the sea arcade to the lower part on the seaward side. The jump is difficult enough to dissuade many opponents from directly following.

The short edges of the map are bounded by a low sea wall, beyond which the fall will kill a character. This wall can be climbed and is an interesting shooting spot.

The courtyard between the arcades has an upper level

Monastery

Spawn

Spawn

Ravine

↑ Town Gate

🌀 Spawn

Lodge

Hollow

Grove

🌀 Spawn

< Cliffside

(dominated by a large cross) next to the wall arcade and a lower level (with gravestones) next to the open arcade. In arena the cross is useful as a shield for bandaging. However archers on the sea arcade can cover both courtyards.

RAVINE

A roughly symmetrical, long conquest map in a wooded valley. Ambient sounds include thunder and birdsong.

The Saxon spawn is backed by a ruined castle. The Cliffside Objective point is at the upper end of the sloping path between two earthworks. The path is the only way up to the Objective point for attackers, although defenders can jump out over the earthworks. The sloping path is slightly narrowed at the lower end by a boulder obtruding into it. This would be the point for a defensive shield wall.

Towards the back of the spawn point there is some above head height cover on either side. On the right a boulder flanked with logs provides a cover but also, on the right, a place for an archer to jump up and shoot between the logs towards the entry path. On the left, a brick wall provides varying height cover as the sides slope up but also they can be used to jump to the top of the wall for longer shots.

The Grove Objective point is outside the Saxon spawn between two cottages with a high path on either side. The left hand path has a wall at the highest point providing a little cover for shooting at the objective. The wider right hand path has a shorter higher wall. Both walls can be jumped onto but there is little point as the height gained does not outweigh the visibility as a target.

There are two large boulders adjacent to the objective, creating more opportunities for cover and for fighting around and behind. Beyond the cottages the path middle path leads between two high rocky shelves, forming a pond bottomed cave on either side. The side paths having briefly dipped, rise again to widen out on the top of the cave roofs. Each has a spur pointing towards the other roof and the gap is jumpable at this point. The Hollow Objective point is directly under the leap.

The ponds are steep and deep but do not cause death and therefore can be used for hiding. The Objective point is protected by barricades at each end of the middle path, providing a little cover for bandaging and for archers.

Beyond the leap the Lodge Objective point lays between two cottages, a high path either side and two boulders in a similar layout to those at the Saxon spawn.

Behind this wooden palisades hold back earthworks on either side while the path through the middle provides the only access to the Town Gate Objective point. Beyond the entrance the high ground has wooden fences providing a bit of cover at either side. The Viking spawn is backed by a wooden fence and gate beyond which can be seen the roofs of a small village.

SANCTUARY

This is a square map with a graveyard theme. There are no jumps or falls that will kill you on this map. Ambient sounds include the cawing of crows, rustling leaves and crackling flames near the torches. The Map is bounded by an unjumpable wall. The spawn ends are almost identical except one is backed by the gable wall of a ruined building and the other has a ruined tower at the corner.

At the centre of the map running parallel to spawn ends is a bridge, broken at both ends before it would exit the map. The bridge is the only place on the map you can have the advantage of height, however it is in line of sight from almost everywhere else on the map, and therefore is

SANCTUARY

Spawn

Spawn

a dangerous place to stand. The Bridge has a ramp up to it on the left side of each spawn. The ramp is a safer place than the bridge for ranged to have a height advantage.

A shallow square moat surrounds the area crossed by the bridge and a middle channel bisects it. The channel runs through the central arch of the bridge. This arch provides a small amount of cover. The channel has sloping sides and therefore can be exited without a jump. Although the moat is shallow it takes a jump to get out, except where there are steps. As a jump results in a momentary pause a player in the moat is at a disadvantage.

Moving across the moat involves the danger of a jump (you are vulnerable at the pause when you land) except at the plank bridges at the spawn ends. A slope leads up from the moat at the "outside edge" of each plank bridge and is therefore the safest point at which to exit the moat.

Between the moat and the wall is a small strip of level ground, wider at the spawn ends and narrower along the perpendicular ends which are interspersed with "buttresses" providing some cover for bandaging.

STRONGHOLD

A map shaped like the infinity symbol ∞, bounded by lakes at either end. The Objective points are all marked by a column of light rising into the sky. The map has an impassable river running through the middle and the only crossing point is the Mead Hall that spans the river. The map is roughly symmetrical with similar important points on either side of the river.

At the first Objective point (South Gate/Lakeside) there are three routes to the rest of the map. On the left a staircase leads up to an upper walkway from which the first/final Objective point (South Gate/Lakeside) can be

Stronghold

Spawn

Lakeside

Blacksmith

Mead Hall

South Gate

Foundry

Spawn

covered. From the walkway your archers can cover the door of the Mead Hall and the area outside. Further along the upper walkway you can jump or walk to the roof of the Foundry/Blacksmith or continue on to the Gallows Steps.

On the right a path through a wall leads slightly up to the spawn point. Form here you can access the roof of the Foundry/Blacksmith.

Alongside the wall of the Foundry/Blacksmith a lower walkway covers the middle path from the final Objective point to the gallows area outside the Mead Hall. Below this the middle path leads around the buildings, past the open doors of the Foundry/Blacksmith to the gallows.

The second Objective point is located within the Foundry/Blacksmith. Between the two open doorways of the Foundry/Blacksmith is a large fire with a lever set next to it. Using the E button to interact with the lever takes three seconds and then a jet of flame shoots from the fire across the Objective point, lasting ten seconds. While the flame is active anyone on any part of the Objective point will take damage, however if you are apparently in the flame but not standing on the Objective point you will not take damage. After the lever is used it takes 40 seconds to reset.

At the back of the foundry a sloping path leads up to the roof. Jumping from the highest part of the roof to the inside of the Foundry/Blacksmith floor will result in death. But jumping from the highest part of the roof to the lowest path area outside is survivable. Jumping from the slopes of the Foundry/Blacksmith roof is survivable.

The gallows area is entered high up from the upper walkway via the gallows steps and at ground level below the walkway via the middle path. On the right is a high area from which you can jump down into the area outside the Mead Hall, or jump onto the top of the fence separating the two areas.

The lower entry continues into a path that slopes up either side of a chopping block to the doorway of the Mead Hall and a fence separating grave area from the gallows.

The Mead Hall has the Objective point in the centre, between the two main doorways. The long axis of the Mead hall has a door at either end leading to a wooden platform over the river. Each side has a small area abutting the two Gallows Areas. As you go out of the Mead Hall river doors each left hand side has a grave and an open fence through which an archer can cover most of the Gallows area and some of the high walkway. The right hand side has high, unjumpable walls. One side has a trough. The trough end also has a grassy slope down to the river. Touching the river is fatal.

TIDE

A roughly oval map of a beach fronted cave. Ambient sounds include rain and thunder. At either edge of the cave a narrow path slopes up and runs around the back edge of the cave. Rock formations provide cover from the rest of the map and between them are approaches to the path. At the centre back of the cave a rock formation has a small ledge around the front from which it is possible to jump to a large rock formation standing in the centre of the cave.

The whole front of the cave opens to the shore where three Viking boats are drawn up. They can all be walked on. Jumping onto each of the two smaller boats on the left needs care as they lie beyond the shallow water in the death depth and jumping over the boats is fatal. The large boat on the right has furled sail down the centre which is not passable. Therefore fighting between either side of the boat is limited to spears and ranged weapons. The far end of the boat is out of area.

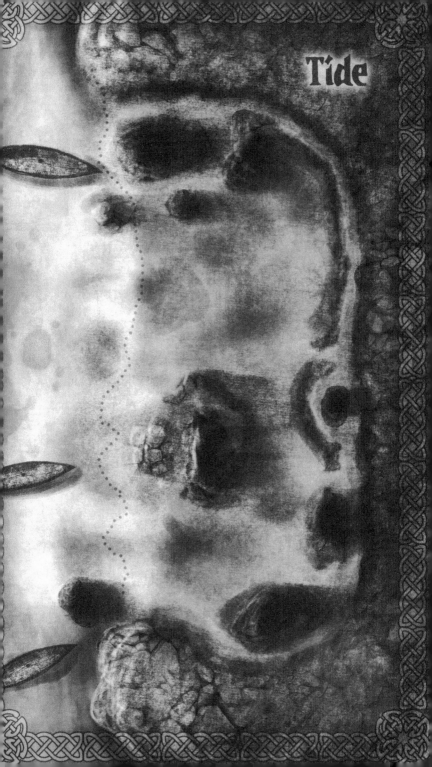

Tide

CHAPTER 7: GLOSSARY

Not sure what an acronym means? Then this is the chapter for you!

1: Can be used to denote "ready".

1H: One-handed. Denotes a weapon held by one hand.

2H: Two-handed. Denotes a weapon held in both hand.

admin: A game server administrator, someone who has the capability to adjust the server settings or to ban/kick players from the server.

afk: Away from keyboard.

aka: Also known as.

atm: At the moment.

ban: To prohibit or deny access. Usually to deny access to a game server.

bbiab: Be back in a bit.

bbl: Be back later.

beta: Trial release meant to test the game and sort out bugs.

brb: Be right back.

brt: Be right there.

btw: By the way.

cap: Capture; denotes taking an Objective.

cba: Can't be arsed.

CD: Cool down; the time it takes before a perk can be used again.

charge time: The time it takes for a weapon strike to build power.

clan: An officially organised team of players that can play other teams.

clan tag: Identifier that goes before or after a player's alias.

core: Fundamental members of a team.

deflection: The concept that weak attacks bounce off of armour.

dev: Game developer.

DoT: Damage over time.

exploiter/abuser: Person who plays unfair using bug.

FF: Friendly fire; damage caused by one's own teammates.

FoV: Field of view, what you can see from a certain point.

FPS: Frames per second.

FPV: First person view.

FS: Fatshark. the Swedish game development studio that made *War of the Vikings*.

ftl: For the loss.

ftw: For the win.

fyi: For your information.

GF: Good fight, used after a fight in which you respect your opponent.

GG: Good game; ending words after a great round.

GJ: Good job.

GL: Good luck.

gtg: Got to go.

GZ or **gratz:** Congratulations.

helicoptering: Using high mouse sensitivity to twirl rapidly.

hit box: Refers to target areas on character models and weapon models. A character model has hit boxes corresponding to different parts of their body. Damage is modified by what hit box weapon attacks land on (head shots do more damage etc.). Weapons also have hit boxes. Swords have hit boxes the size of their entire blades. Axes and pole arms have hit boxes limited to the actual head/tip of the weapon.

HP: Health points.

HUD: Heads up display.

IAS: Increased attack speed.

IC: I see.

IDC: I don't care.

IDK: I don't know.

IIRC: If I remember correctly.

IK: I know.

IMBA: Imbalanced.

IMHO: In my honest/humble opinion.

IMS: Increased movement speed.

IRL: In real life.

J/K: Just kidding.

kk: Okay.

K/D ratio: Kill/Death ratio; your score of kills (frags) versus your deaths (knock-downs/insta-kills). 1:1 is considered a decent K/D ratio. If it's a lot lower it is considered a bad K/D ratio and a higher ratio is considered to be very good.

KS: Kill Steal; habit of finishing enemies while they are fighting with your allies and are already heavily damaged; doing it with purpose to get better K/D ratio.

L2P: Learn to play.

LMAO: Laughing my ass off.

LMB: Left mouse button.

LOL: Laughing out loud.

LVL: Level.

merc: Mercenary; someone who plays with a team or clan while not actually belonging to them.

mIRC: IRC client (http://www.mirc.com).

MMB: Middle mouse button.

Mod: Moderator.

n1: Nice one.

np: No problem.

NTY: No thank you.

PM: Private message.

PoS: Parent(s) over shoulder.

pub: Public game; a game/server open to anyone (as opposed to a pass worded server).

OMG: Oh my gosh.

OMW: On my way.

OIC: Oh I see.

OP: Overpowered; weapon that is considered to have unfair advantage.

ORLY: Oh really.

PDX: Paradox; the Swedish game publisher that commissioned *War of the Vikings*.

QFT: Quoted for truth.

QQ: Crying.

randomer: Someone who randomly attacks other players on a duel server.

randoming: Randomly attacking other players on a duel server.

rdy: Ready.

res/rez: Resurrect.

RMB: Right mouse button.

RNG: Random number generator often used to indicate randomness in general.

ROFL: Rolling on the floor laughing.

sec: Give me a second, Often in response to "rdy?".

SFX: Sound effects.

spammer: Generic term for a player who throws out a high volume of attacks. Usually used to refer to high speed bows that shoot rapidly, or to melee fighters who attack continuously without parrying.

spamming: Throwing out a high volume of attacks. Often used to refer to high speed bows that shoot rapidly, or to melee fighters who attack continuously without parrying.

ss: Screen shot.

SSAO: Screen Space Ambient Occlusion.

swing speed: The speed at which a melee weapon is swung. Can refer to the amount of time it takes for an attack to charge, but more often refers to how fast the swing travels after being released.

TBH: To be honest.

THX/TY: Thanks/Thank you.

TLDR: Too long; didn't read.

TS: Teamspeak; a voice chat program.

TTYL: Talk to you later.

TY: Thank you.

TYT: Take your time.

TYVM: Thank you very much.

UI: User Interface.

UP: Underpowered; a weapon that is considered to have unfair disadvantage.

Vent: Ventrilo; a voice chat program.

WASD: The directional movement keyboard keys.

WB: Welcome back.

WC: Wrong chat/conversation

WP: Well played.

XP/EXP: Experience points.

YT: You there?

YW: You're welcome.

ACKNOWLEDGEMENTS

It is the fate of game guides of this kind to be out of date before they appear, due to the constant refinement of the game by the devoted developers. We expect this one to be no different. However, we hope to be able to make some updates and would therefore be grateful for any constructive criticism or corrections.

We would like to thank Tomas Härenstam, for offering us the opportunity to write this manual and for his help and encouragement while guiding us through the process.

We are indebted to members of Fatshark and Paradox Interactive for their help and advice, especially Robin Hagblom, John Rickne, Liam O'Neill, Adam Timèn and Daniel Platt.

As always we are thankful to the clan members of Guard of Istiniar [IG] for their cheerfully and unstintingly giving up many hours of play time to help us test seemingly meaningless little details, although they had no idea why we were doing it. We are also greatly indebted to the many members of the community who gave up play time to help test in public servers.

ABOUT THE AUTHORS

Both Aeronwen and Lisen have considerable experience of working in education. As leaders in the gaming clan Guard of Istiniar [IG] they have used their educational expertise to further the clan's emphasis on training basic skills and team play. IG, famously, has no skill requirement for members but recruits on character alone, believing that respect for teammates and fellow players is the bedrock of a good team player, upon which skill can be built.

Lisen has shown his exceptional ability to self-coach, becoming one of the finest players in first *Warband*, then *War of the Roses,* where he was the first player to reach level 60, and now in *War of the Vikings.* In addition to his capacity for understanding the game sufficiently to be a pre-eminent player in all classes and with all weapons, Lisen has an aptitude for instruction. His personal qualities which have gained him the trust and respect of the gaming community are also those that enable him to be one of the finest gameplay coaches.

Aeronwen is (thanks to Lisen's coaching abilities) a competent player whose organisational skills and attention to detail have been utilised in clan management and the writing of this manual.

PART II: THE HISTORY

WELCOME TO ENGLAND AD870

Anglo-Saxon England – AD870 – welcomes careful spear carriers! This is no joke. Carry your spear level, and if somebody runs into it, they only have themselves to blame. Wave it around point up and if it sticks somebody, you'll end up paying them, and the local king, compensation … unless you are a stranger or an outlaw, at which point things may go very badly for you. (Expect the Vikings to have similar rules.)

While keeping your spear on the level, and avoiding leaving the King's Highway (we'll come to that), take a deep breath … fill your lungs with the clean preindustrial air – unless, that is, you're standing downwind of a charcoal burners settlement, or wandering the rubbish-strewn streets of a reeking town.

However, even the pollutants smell different. You're not in the 21st century any more. It's not even called "England". That's just a geographical term like modern "North America". Well, slightly more than a mere geographical term: England is the region of Britain settled by the Anglo-Saxons.

The Anglo-Saxons are a Northern European Germanic people like the Vikings. Like the Vikings they first came to Britain as raiders, preying on the crumbling carcass of Roman Britain. When the Roman commander took the legions away to make himself – briefly – an emperor, the native Celtic Britons were left to defend themselves from the raiders. They did fine until some bright spark decided to hire Anglo-Saxons to fight the Anglo-Saxons. Within a hundred years the former Roman province of Britain became a collection of Anglo-Saxon kingdoms making up England. As for the Britons, some of them fled to Wales. However the Anglo-Saxon term for the Welsh can also mean "slave", which should give us a clue.

(*Anglo-Saxon: These early invaders were actually made up of several different tribes plus hangers on including Angles, Saxons, Jutes, Danes, and Franks. By the 9th century, scholars had lumped them together and called them Anglo-Saxons, so that's the term we'll use.*)

By AD870, some of the Anglo-Saxon kingdoms have eaten their neighbours and become rather bloated. From top to bottom we have:

Northumberland (Northumbrians) stretches from the Firth of Forth in modern Scotland down to the Humber River. It used to be a cradle of learning and culture. Now it's occupied by the Vikings who rule from the city of Yorvic (modern York).

Mercia (Mercians) is the fat middle kingdom. It once dominated the island, now it's a coweringly "neutral" land corridor for rapacious Viking armies.

Wessex (West Saxons) lies across the bottom of the island. Its royal brothers, King Ethelred and Alfred, are still heroically holding off the Vikings. Alfred will be known to later history as "the Great".

Essex (East Saxons) and East Anglia (East Anglians), small kingdoms off to the east, utterly overrun by Vikings.

ENGLAND
IN THE
NINTH CENTURY

KINGDOM OF PICTS

DÁL RIATA

Dumbarton
Clut

STRATHCLYDE

NORTHUMBRIA

Tweed

IRELAND

Dublin

WALES

MERCIA

Nottingham

Trent

Severn

EAST ANGLIA

Wye

ESSEX

London

Thames

Reading

WESSEX

Winchester

KENT

WALES

Kent (Jutes) is the heel of Wessex, but hasn't been an independent kingdom in living memory, being first invaded by Mercia then Wessex. These days, it's solidly Viking.

By now you've noticed that England has a bad case of Vikings. The Vikings came as raiders, discovered weakness and became invaders and settlers. And of course the raiding continues. For the first time in centuries, the land is divided between Christians and Heathens; the Vikings still worship the Germanic gods long abandoned by the Anglo-Saxons.

*(**Vikings:** The Anglo-Saxons mostly call the Scandinavian invaders Norwegians or Danes, but use the terms interchangeably. Since some of them are also Swedes, and, by AD870, many of them were actually born and bred in the British Isles, We'll stick to calling them Vikings, a term originally reserved for pirates.)*

CHRISTIAN ANGLO-SAXONS

As you stroll through 9th-century England (still carrying your spear with care, I hope!) you'll notice that Christian monuments pin down the landscape; crosses, chapels, churches, cathedrals, and monasteries–in Viking occupied areas, some of these may show signs of fire damage, but most will still be operating.

If you watch carefully, you'll catch the English following old pagan customs; folksy stuff like decorating trees, corn dollies and making wishes at holy wells. You'll also overhear traditional prayers that reek of magic, and catch explicitly magical charms doing the rounds.

Even so, the Anglo-Saxons call themselves Christian. Most areas have been Christian for at least two hundred years. This is very much a Christian country, which – as we shall see – is not always a good thing.

In AD870, Christian means "Catholic", but people don't

bandy around the term because as far as they are concerned, there is only one kind of Christianity. The churches of East and West won't split for another two centuries. Right now the East obeys Constantinople (modern Istanbul), the capital of the Byzantine Empire. The West, including England, obeys Rome, now a city state surrounded by warring kingdoms and independent cities. But though they argue over who is top dog, the Pope of Rome and the Patriarch of Constantinople still belong to the same church.

This makes international diplomacy easy for English kings, especially when making trade treaties. The downside is that some of the wealth of the kingdom flows to Rome.

(*Heresies: Other flavours of Christianity – "heresies" – have existed in the past. They usually hinge on whether or not Jesus was God, or Man, or both at the same time and in what manner. The big heresies around her were Arianism amongst Germanic peoples, and Pelagianism in Britain. However, the Anglo-Saxons barbarians who settled in Britain at the end of the Roman Empire were Heathens; a blank slate for missionaries. And as for Pelagianism – this was the heresy of the Roman Britons. Thanks to the Anglo-Saxons, you don't see them about any more.*)

Though thoughtful churchmen might say otherwise, for ordinary Anglo-Saxons, Christianity is all about not making God angry; You wouldn't like God when he's angry; he sends things like plagues and barbarian invaders (hint). For this reason it's really important for the kingdom, not just the individual, that everybody have a priest to look to for religious guidance, and of course to carry out the rites that keep God happy.

In practice, this means the countryside is divided up into parishes, each the responsibility of one or more priests. Sometimes worship takes place at a cross in a field and the priest is based at a grand "minister", a large church with a commune of priests and perhaps a monastery. More usually these days, there's a church built by the local lord and the priest is part of the community. Sometimes the church us just a cross in a field with a visiting priest.

We don't really know what the priests are like. If it's anything like later history, a priest can be anything from a community leader, through to the local sex pest.

The religious role of a priest gives him the potential to be part social worker, part therapist. He welcomes people into the Church with the rite of baptism, cleanses the soul by hearing Confession and apportioning penances, blesses marriages at the church door, gives the dying their Last Rites and performs the Funeral Rites when they will be tucked up in their graves to await for the Last Judgement, the only one that matters since nobody has thought to invent Purgatory to patch the gap between death and Resurrection.

In some ways, the Christian world view is a cosy one. At each stage of their life, the Church is there to give comfort and certainty, and if there are deficiencies in this life, that's OK because the next one will be a lot better.

The downside is that all this is compulsory. The Last Judgement is a judgement and people expect it to be a bit like a tick box questionnaire; *"Were you baptized? No? BZZZZZ Straight to Hell. Attend mass regularly? Just how often? Too bad. BZZZZZ!"*

This makes for a certain grimness around the edges. It's just one of those things if the local priest is too sick to baptise your dying baby, or if your wife commits suicide, or if you die in battle without having made your confession.

It also means that the priest can hold a giant theological gun to your head. All those comforting rites and rituals come with a price tag, gifts and fees. The priest probably gets rent from a chunk of the village land and there's also the tithe – a tenth of your yearly produce that goes to support the priest. It's still legally voluntary, but good luck with avoiding it.

To aid them in this, the priests have morality cookbooks called penitentials. These give a bewildering list of sins and prescribe penances, usually some kind of fasting – more of a boring diet than starvation – for weeks, months, years, even, and a public declaration of penance.

A good proportion of the sins are sexual – anything that's not baby-making man-wife sex with the man on top is a sin. The same goes for having sex on holy days, within three days of getting married, on a Wednesday or a Friday, or during daylight hours. And, God forbid – literally – that you should see your wife naked.

Needless to say, "charitable" donations could stand in for all that fasting, so the loves and lusts of the parish must have been a nice earner for an unscrupulous priest.

There's also the issue of priests and sex.

Priests are supposed to be celibate, in part to stop the role becoming hereditary. However, priests are wealthy by local standards, young and often from noble backgrounds. They also have plenty of time on their hands. And they spend an awful lot of time listening to other people going into the juicy details of their sex lives…

Judging from the way the Church is always harping on about clerical celibacy, you can expect many Anglo-Saxon priests to have girlfriends, mistresses and even wives, sometimes all at the same time. This is a bad thing for both the ladies involved and their kin.

Legitimate marriage brings families together and through alliance makes them both stronger. It also confers status on the bride, and ensures the future of any offspring. A relationship with a priest brings none of these benefits. However, most peasant fathers and brothers will not be able to kick up a fuss about this because the chances are that the priest has the backing of the local lord.

Not only did the local lord probably build the church, he quite likely owns it. He gets to pick the priest – a great gig for a younger brother or illegitimate offspring. He also expects a rake-off from all those pious gifts and fees, and sees nothing at all wrong with this.

Churches take fees and tithes from everybody in the parish, not just from the tenants of the local lord. This is a great way to extract money and gain influence over any free farmers who own their own land or rent it from somebody else.

Founding a church is often a blatant tax dodge. Churches don't pay tax. A lord can put his tithe into it and get some of the money back from the priest, who may also work for him as an unpaid clerk. Talking of tax dodges, the local lord might be an abbot for purely tax purposes. In the last century, this has become a headache for kings wanting to raise money to pay for things like armies.

The problem is that anybody with the money and land can found a monastery. The new institution can follow any set of rules, no matter how odd or corrupt. The countryside must be littered with deserted or dying small monasteries that seemed "a good idea at the time" to some rich noble in the throes of a midlife crisis, or some well-heeled youth in the grip of a religious enthusiasm.

The big monasteries, and the ministers where the bishops base themselves, provide Anglo-Saxon England's education system. Without them, there would be no clerks to record down laws and keep tax records, nobody to write and read communications. In a few years, King Alfred of Wessex will try to have all his officials learn to read, and he will need the Church for that as well.

Even so, the monasteries and ministers together probably do a kingdom more harm than good.

The Church is always buying or being given land. However, the Church never goes bust, never sells land, never dies. So, over time, more and more land is Church land, exempt from paying taxes or supplying soldiers.

How are the Anglo-Saxon kings supposed to reward their best warriors if they have no land to give them?

The Church is glad enough of the protection of rough men with weapons, but whines and complains whenever a king takes away land in order to support his army.

Back in the last century, the Venerable Bede, an influential Northumbrian churchman, complained about the fake monasteries that were taking up land, making it hard for the King of Northumberland to retain ambitious soldiers and thus weakening the kingdom.

Judging from the way the Vikings gobbled up Northumberland it's clear that it wasn't just the fake monasteries that were sapping the military might of the English kings.

By AD870, though a pious Christian will not admit it, the Church has reaped what it has sewn. Its greed has undermined the capacity of the local kings to defend the resulting wealth. The Heathen Vikings have come.

HEATHEN VIKINGS

Nearly a hundred years ago, back in AD793, the Vikings started ransacking monasteries, slaughtering or enslaving the monks. The Vikings are notorious Heathens, so the Church, of course, got hysterical about a War on Christianity.

However, looking back from war-torn AD870, we can see that the Vikings aren't so much *anti-Christian* as *pro-pillage*.

Right from the start, the Vikings were quite happy to

let the locals buy back stolen holy books, and they preferred enslaving monks to slaying them.

True, a Viking queen did once perform Heathen rites on the altar of an Irish monastery, however when the Vikings settle, they tend to live and let live.

Plenty of churches survive in the shadow of the Heathen strongholds of Yorvic and far-off Dublin. Viking Yorvic even has a Christian Archbishop. It's no wonder, because in Northumberland, the Vikings have become the overlords of the local English nobility who turn out to be quite happy to follow them to war. Late-coming Vikings looking for land end up settling on marginal patches of heath or hill; overlords don't displace their people.

The Vikings, you see, are a bit like Robert E Howard's Conan; they believe in the existence of the Gods and magic, but don't automatically accord them any special reverence. For example, the funeral poem of Harold the Good describes him arriving in Odin's hall with his slain men and deciding to keep his weapons handy; *One should not trust the King of the Gods!*

A Viking can have a relationship with a God, but it looks a lot like the kind of voluntary relationship you might have with a chieftain; *You look after me, I'll serve you.*

Unlike the Anglo-Saxons, and the rest of Christian Europe, the Vikings don't seem to have an organised caste of professional priests, or any kind of religious hierarchy.

That said, priestesses, witches and seeresses pop up from time to time. These can be actual Viking queens and highborn women, like Queen Ota who once prophesied from the altar of a burning Irish monastery. They can also be in-house specialists, such as the Angel of Death described by an Arab traveller. Typically, however, they seem to be odd old women who travel from place-to-place.

Even if religious professionals do exist, public religion

is something leaders take charge of. Kings and chieftains sacrifice to Odin. Farmers and landowners (who can also be chieftains), typically sacrifice to Thor. Both maintain temples, sometimes actual buildings, but more often a sacred grove or even a single tree.

Private religious practice has a do-it-yourself feel and is hard to tell apart from magic; a prayer for healing, love or luck in battle, for example, citing the deeds of heroes and gods; *Just as Thor smote the giants, may I smite my enemies.*

The Vikings are a pragmatic lot. Even the Gods cannot avoid Fate, and actions now will have tragic consequences later. So, though the Vikings believe in the supernatural realm, they approach it in a matter-of-fact way.

There were certainly practitioners of black magic, but the three socially acceptable ways of dealing with the supernatural:

Runes, given to the Vikings by Odin (or developed after contact with the more civilised Romans and Greeks). This is an alphabet designed to be easy to carve into stone and wood. You'll find Viking scratchings as far afield as Greece: *Olaf was here.*

Runes are great for naming swords and writing on grave slabs. However, they can also be used for magic. Please get the spelling right or a love charm can make the target sick instead.

Sacrifice. Vikings definitely sacrificed animals to their Gods. They probably also sacrificed humans. The alleged deaths of King Edmund of Kent and King Aelle of Northumberland's both have the feel of religious ritual. We also have high status graves that seem to include slaves sacrificed to keep their owner company in the afterlife, and an Arab description of this happening.

Prophecy, usually supplied by a woman, either an amateur of high status, or an itinerant seeress, sometimes with her own team of all-singing all-dancing attendants.

Battle Magic, for which the evidence is flakier, included pre-battle dancing, tossing a spear over the opposing army, and going into a "berserk" trance state.

All these ways of approaching the supernatural do so with reference to the Viking Gods. We only really know about these mythological figures and their world from later or hostile sources, plus the odd archaeological find. Here's the picture:

The Viking Gods live in *Asgard*, connected to our world – *Midgard* – via the rainbow *Bifrost Bridge*. They comprise two tribes who once fought each other: the *Aesir*, a rough-and-tumble bunch; and the more grounded *Vanir*, who seem focused on fertility and farming.

Odin the Allfather, the one-eyed spear-carrying King of the Gods and God of War. He gives and takes away victory, is not to be trusted, and generally prefers his sacrificial victims hanged and stabbed. He possibly also enjoys a good blood eagle – a ritual in involving tearing out the victim's lungs so they flap amusingly – though modern scholars still debate whether this is real.

Odin is also god of Magic, especially the Runes. He traded his eye for the Runes in a bizarre upside down hanging ritual, rides a six legged horse (a visual pun on the traditional six-handled bier used to transport corpses), and thanks to a pair of ravens and a magic throne is a kind of one-god NSA.

His female helpers, the *Valkyries,* also known as "Choosers of the Slain", gather the souls of elite warriors from battlefields and take them to the Odin's hall, *Valhalla,* for an afterlife of feasting, fighting and wenching. These ladies aren't the buxom sword-chicks in chainmail corsets and winged helmets we see in modern films and comics. It's not clear that they actually fight, and they are sometimes seen working at a loom weaving entrails. Possibly, real Valkyries exist and are simply priestesses of Odin. Who knows, maybe some of them do fight?

Tyr, One-Handed God of War overlaps Odin's role. Both Gods' stories seem muddled, for example each featuring a suspiciously similar wolf. (Tyr certainly seems to be the older of the two, his worship going back to Roman times.) However, Tyr is also a lawgiver and we can see him as more of a soldier god, for example willingly sacrificing his hand to bind Fenris the Wolf (a long story).

Being a soldier god does not necessarily make Tyr benign. The kind of soldiering he represents comes from a time when war and ethnic cleansing were indistinguishable. In the old days, a typical sacrifice to Tyr might involve taking all your prisoners of war, hanging them upside down from trees and slitting their noses so that their blood drains into pots.

Thor, Red-Bearded Thunder God is another fighting god, but very much of the home-defence type. Armed with *Mjolnir*, a self-guided reusable throwing hammer, he spends most of his time killing any giants who threaten Asgard. Vikings quite like to wear miniature hammers, much like Christian crosses, and often swear oaths on a sacred ring or armband dedicated to Thor.

Because he controls the weather, Thor is popular with sailors, which is perhaps why he has both a temple and a sacred grove at Dublin. A temple dedicated to Thor could be huge structure complete with a statue on a cart for worshippers to pull as a kind of ritual service. Some Viking houses incorporated two pillars carved with images of Thor, with nails banged in for striking fire. Settlers often carried these with them, sometimes tossing them overboard and picking their settlement site according to where these washed up.

Loki, God of Mischief, is the archetypal pain-in-the-ass.

Unlike most trickster gods, Loki's spiteful pranks have caused real harm, including the death of Baldur, and a manufacturing flaw in Thor's hammer that has left it a little too short in the handle for the safe slaying of poisonous mega-serpents. Loki is also responsible for setting in motion Ragnarok, the inevitable doom of the Gods.

It's not clear that anybody actually worships Loki. There certainly isn't much point: as of some unspecified time in the mythological past, the Gods condemned Loki to be imprisoned in a lonely cave, chained over spiky rocks with a snake dripping venom into his face, and there he still is.

If you experience an earthquake, that's Loki's wife changing the cup she uses to catch the poison. The god is writhing in his chains. Don't worry, he won't get free any time soon.

Loki's fate probably tells us something about the Viking attitude towards people who don't take life seriously enough.

Freyja, Goddess of Love, Fertility and Magic. Big on unbridled carnality, she can turn into a horse to enjoy equestrian frolics. Though a Vanir (all the above gods are Aesir), she may be chief of Odin's Valkyries, and has her own hall to which half of the slain heroes go, as do virtuous women.

Freyja is the patron of the itinerant female shamanic seers, often called "spae wives" or "volvas". These fur wearing ladies are reputed to go around in groups of nine, but are more likely to be encountered solo. If one arrives at your home, put her in a high seat and find maidens to help with the singing. She'll go into a trance and supply prophecies. You can also ask her to help with minor magics, but avoid insulting her by implying she can do black magic … she might be tempted to give you a very personal demonstration.

White Christ. No, this isn't a joke. The Vikings were "polytheistic" – recognise multiple gods – so have no problem with finding a spot for Christ in their temples. Nor do they wipe out all traces of Christianity when they find it. Remember, Yorvic has kept its archbishop, and the churches around Viking Dublin survive and thrive.

Vikings are usually happy to undergo "prime signing" – marking with holy water as a first step towards full baptism. However, they are less keen on rejecting their traditional gods and attempts to properly convert them tend to produce as many martyred priests as Viking converts.

In the years to come, the Vikings will become Christians. But they will picture Christ as a young warrior, understand his crucifixion as being like Odin's grisly self-sacrifice and will fail to apply the "love thy neighbour" message any further than their actual neighbours. For example, one miracle of St Olaf – an early Viking saint – involves him interceding in a Viking-on-Viking battle over loot garnered from raiding both sides of the Irish Sea.

There are of course lots of other gods including *Heimdal*, blind guardian of the Bifrost Bridge, *Ran*, goddess of the sea, and *Baldur* who may, or may not, be a dying fertility god. *Giants, Monsters* and *Dwarves* lurk on the edge of the cosmos, which is draped over the various levels of *Yggdrasil the World Tree*. Odin and his brothers created the world by dismembering Ymir the Giant, and it will be giants and monsters – mostly sired by Gods – who bring about the end of the world in one vast battle, *Ragnarok*.

Even so, the Vikings are not so very different from the Anglo-Saxons they are fighting.

GERMANIC COUSINS

We moderns expect the Vikings and the Anglo-Saxons to be different. It's easy to take a bloodthirsty Viking saga and contrast it with – say – an English monk musing on the changing seasons. However, that's comparing the thoughts of a warrior with those of a holy man.

In a sense, the Vikings are victims of their own success. In the early Middle Ages, they are great warriors and courageous navigators, so come to England as raiders and invaders. Not exactly good PR!

In the 12th century, having converted to Christianity, the Vikings will become unusually literate. Gentlemen scholars will rush to capture the tales of their heroic ancestors, and since the interesting stories revolve around fighting, burning and pillaging, that's what we get in the sagas.

Meanwhile, there are only a handful of detailed accounts of the war from the Anglo-Saxon point of view, and, since the Anglo-Saxons are the defenders, these stories are high on heroics, low on atrocities against civilian populations.

However, the English haven't always been the virtuous defenders, nor will they always be. Until the Vikings came, the English kingdoms mostly fought each other … when they weren't invading their Celtic neighbours in Cornwall, Wales and Pictland, or having civil wars, of course. War in this era mostly means ravaging an opponent's lands and slaughtering his peasants in the hope that he will submit or rush to battle and be defeated.

When you adjust for the different stances – defender and invader – you can immediately see that the English and the Vikings have very similar lives and cultures, and thus similar characters.

This should be no surprise, since they are both Germanic peoples.

A Viking like Egil Skallagrimsson can burn old people in their bed, reduce peasants to poverty with his raids, and still write a heartbreaking poem on the death of his son. Anglo-Saxon kings can lay waste to their neighbour's territory and came to found a church or endow a monastery.

Meanwhile, the cosy farming communities of both cultures have scrupulous rules for paying just the right amount of compensation to avoid a feud, but cheerfully beat their slaves, execute outlaws and suspected witches, and no-doubt rob strangers when they can get away from it.

These are good people getting by in a harsh world.

Just as the divide between surviving and perishing is sharp and distinct, so, for them is the divide between people and not-people. *People* you treat fairly and with empathy. *Not-people* you treat according to custom, which may not turn out so well for them.

Strangers aren't people, nor are slaves.

Acquaintances and neighbours can be people.

That's why both Vikings and Anglo-Saxons go to such effort to establish emotional bonds through fostering of young children, marriage alliance, and gift giving between lord and follower; *Don't be a stranger. Seriously.*

So when, in AD870, you travel through England you'll find more similarities than not between Anglo-Saxon and Viking regions.

TRAVEL

You can make good progress crossing England. Expect to cover 25 to 40 kilometers a day on foot, perhaps twice that on horseback.

The old Roman roads mark the best overland routes, carry English names like "Watling Street" and "Ermine

Street", and were constructed by legendary heroes, giants and (cough) Gods. The centuries have worn them down. In many places they are just a braid of tracks. Even so, there are recognisable "highways" and local lords have the duty to maintain river crossings and patch up the worst of the potholes. There are also the ancient ridgeways, traditional tracks following the tops of upland ridges.

Whatever you do, don't leave the road. If you do, Anglo-Saxons will assume you are a robber and kill you on general principle. True, you can blow a horn or shout to demonstrate your good intentions, but that's likely to attract real robbers, including the perhaps the locals who will deny they heard anything before they shot you and took your possessions.

And, of course, if the locals are Vikings, you had better have a very good reason for encroaching on their territory.

The same goes for arriving by water.

You can make up to 150 kilometers a day in a longship at sea, assuming pirates or storms don't get you, and perhaps half that going upstream on a river.

In the old days, when you came ashore, a reeve would ride up to ask you your business and levy a tax. These days, everybody is understandably a bit jumpy, so be careful where you land and try not to look like raiders (especially if you are raiders).

The thing you notice as you travel around this pre-modern landscape is that people live here, it all belongs to somebody.

It's not like Middle Earth – well.

OK, to the Vikings, this is all "Middle Earth", Midgard. What I really mean is England is not like Tolkien's Middle Earth. It's not empty, with vast deserted spaces created by war in times gone by.

Instead, in England AD870, you're never far from people. Each site where a village could thrive already has a village. All the cultivatable ground is cultivated.

Those greenwoods are managed for game, timber and grazing. The local lord owns the hunting. The lesser folk meanwhile jealously guard their rights to gathering fallen firewood and pasturing their pigs.

True, beyond the cultivated fields lie meadows and then moorland, but that's pasture with strict rules about the size of flocks and herds and who can put his animals onto the land.

The same applies to rivers and streams; don't expect to settle down to an afternoon's fishing without getting into trouble.

It's owned for a reason. Almost every part of the landscape is part of somebody's delicately balanced livelihood. There is no space to slot in peaceful settlers. Presumably that's why the Vikings always arrive armed.

The other thing you notice is that long-haul travel is not routine.

On the road you'll meet professional warriors looking for gigs, lords and government officials going about their business, pilgrims who may even be on the way to Rome (the women often end up as prostitutes somewhere in Italy), merchants and itinerant story tellers…

However, these are all the exception. Most of the population stays put unless dragged off for war. That's why there are no inns except perhaps in the larger towns. Instead you are thrown onto people's hospitality.

Travellers are rare enough that hospitality is a pleasant duty for noblemen who will gladly open their halls to those with tales of the wider world to share, and perhaps appropriate presents to make – though don't ever treat this as a commercial transaction.

The lesser folk in their long house may also welcome

you, but more cautiously. The host is legally responsible for the guest. If you do something foolish, they may end up paying the bill.

Monasteries also welcome guests; abbots are not so dissimilar from other rich landlords. They are also supposed to dispense Christian charity, so if you're down on your luck head for a spire and the sound of male singing. This may also work in Viking areas. Though monasteries will have probably been pillaged, they haven't necessarily been wiped out.

If you can't find a monastery, look for charity in the hall of an Anglo-Saxon lord. However, don't go begging at the gate of a Viking warlord. Vikings, you see, have a tradition of castrating beggars.

Though people can and do travel across England AD870, don't expect the locals to extend much trust to strangers. This is in part because that's how people in small rural communities usually are, even in the 21st century. However it's also because of how the law works.

LAW

The laws of the land – both Viking and Anglo-Saxon – are not so much about right and wrong as a system for throwing money at grievances in order to avert the messy business of feud – the tradition whereby two families engage in tit-for-tat killings until one of them gathers up the courage and resources to eliminate the other.

There are strict rules of liability for everything. Did you cut down somebody else's tree? Chop off his finger? Injure his servant? Accidentally stab somebody with a spear? Steal an item?

Don't worry. As long as you have the money to pay up and you are not a slave or an outlaw, then you need not fear the lash or the gallows. You will owe somebody precisely calculated compensation. Of course, if you can't pay, expect to be beaten or hanged, or outlawed… and then you are fair game for anybody who gets a clear shot at you.

Though the Vikings prefer to negotiate compensation on a case by case basis, the English like to write things down. We still have detailed tables of misdeeds and compensation for Anglo-Saxon England.

These include lists of *weregild*, "man gold", standard compensation owed for killing different people. For example, in Mercia, a freeman was worth 200 shillings and a nobleman 1200 shillings.

They also include compensation for specific misdeeds. For example, if you have a drunken fallout with your mate and he keeps cool, then you may need to pay him 30 shillings.

This doesn't sound so bad until you realise that one shilling would buy you a sheep: *You just threw away your entire flock of sheep!*

On the face of it, these laws seem impractical.

Do Anglo-Saxons really live in constant fear of losing their livelihood due to accidentally giving some slight?

Probably not.

It's unlikely that ordinary freemen ever pay such steep fines. We can hope that the courts – usually juries of local people who can't read such lists anyway – have a free hand to set more realistic fines depending on status. It's certainly known for compensation for injuries to be based on a proportion of weregild.

However, two other things may be at work.

First, the compensation is probably paid off in instalments over a very long period, much like a modern credit card bill. Turning a troublemaker into a debtor is a great way of controlling him.

Second, kin – extended families – and lords probably get involved. Kin pool resources to pay off fines. Lords settle the debts of their servants (and then probably give them a beating instead). Both do deals to offset one fine against another: *I drunkenly insulted your cousin, but you cut timber on my uncle's land... My servant punched your servant, but your other servant seduced my wife's maid.*

This gives both your kin and your lords – if you have one – an interest in maintaining your good behaviour; *That bar brawl? It never happened because your brother and third cousin pulled you away.*

Given all this, it's quite sensible for both Anglo-Saxons and Vikings to be wary of strangers.

They don't know who you are. They can't know whether it's safe to trust you, and if you do misbehave or turn out to be an outlaw, then your hosts will be legally responsible for your actions.

Since they don't know who you are, they therefore don't know whether you can afford to pay compensation if you harm them in some way. Sure, paupers and slaves who can't pay are subject to beatings and hangings. But to a poor man who has lost an eye, or a son, or cattle, that's small comfort compared to cash in hand.

Finally, if you are a stranger that means you have no lord or kin to keep you in line.

No surprise then that if you are suspected of a crime, you are in deep trouble. It gets worse. The local court meets regularly – every four weeks seems typical – at some handy landmark. It could be a purpose built enclosure, could be an old stone circle.

The court is a general meeting of all the freemen of the local area, the Anglo-Saxon "hundred" or the Viking "wapentake", drawn from perhaps a couple of hundred families.

The court acts like a community council, sorting out local issues and negotiating with the powers that be. Naturally, it's the government's point of contact for raising tax and soldiers, and for getting the bridges and roads maintained.

The court also chooses juries to hear legal cases.

So far this sounds quite modern. However, though we might hope that jurors will ask questions about evidence, mostly everything rests on your reputation.

There's nothing preventing the jurors from considering hearsay and rumour. Worse, the witnesses are mostly character witnesses: your mates swear that you aren't a thief, your accuser's mates swear that he would not lie like that.

So, if you are a stranger, good luck.

Anglo-Saxon women can generally attend the court – they call it the "moot" – whereas Viking women need somebody to speak for them at the local "thing". Beyond that, women of both societies have similar legal status. They can own property, repudiate the actions of their husbands, make wills and separate from obnoxious spouses.

This seems odd at first, since society seems geared up to treat women as brittle chattels.

WOMEN

Anglo-Saxons and Vikings both are big on extravagant, booze-fuelled feasts. However, these are men's affairs. The women flit in and out of the smoky hall bearing food and drink. If you are an honoured guest, expect your host's wife to fill your cup at least once and for God's (or Odin's) sake, don't pinch her bottom!

This exclusion seems sexist until one is reminded that kindergarten teachers don't sit down to eat with their charges either.

The atmosphere is something like a modern rugby club pub crawl; loud-talking jocks enjoying drinking games and rough sports while the tone of conversation spirals into the gutter. The women, meanwhile, are happy to retire to the more civilised bower, the women's quarters where they can gossip and joke on their own terms, and probably down copious quantities of mead.

Similarly, there at lots of laws that seem to treat women as property: don't attempt to seduce an unmarried daughter, don't run off with another man's wife or romp with his slave (the Vikings will even get cross if you compose a poem to a pretty girl). Worse, compensation for rape or abduction tends to go to the male kin or lord.

However, these laws belong to a pre-contraception era when unwanted pregnancy can bring death or social disaster, and when "seduction" – from the male point of view – does not always require consent, and rape is almost always impossible to prove. The compensation system at least offers some protection by making it in the self-interest of some men to act as protectors; better than nothing, but don't for one moment imagine that these ancient times are in any way a paradise for women.

We've already seen that Viking women can't speak at the Thing, but Anglo-Saxons can say their piece at the local Moot. However, on balance, it's probably better to be a Viking free woman than an Anglo-Saxon one.

The Anglo-Saxon church is using Old Testament thinking to erode the rights of native wives; *Want to "chastise" your wife with a stick? That's fine with the local priest. Is your husband playing around? Too bad. Are YOU playing around? Penance time…*

Meanwhile, the general lawlessness of Viking society works in favour of a Viking wife. It increases her value as a household manager since her husband will often be away.

It also makes it dangerous to mistreat her since she may have well-armed brothers who feel protective over her, if only because they lose face if you beat her up.

In England it works the other way around at the top. The settled Anglo-Saxons have been known to accept a widowed queen as ruler. The Vikings pick their rulers first and foremost on their ability as warlords, so we don't see any female ones.

In the religious sphere, there's a lot more equivalence. Viking women turn up as witches and seeresses, sometimes as independent operators with their own handmaidens. Well-born Anglo-Saxon women who become nuns can rise to the rank of abbess, and that can mean being in charge of mixed establishment of both monks and nuns.

Viking women, like their 19th-century American pioneer counterparts, are certainly happy and able to pick up weapons in home defence. However, we don't know that Anglo-Saxon women don't do this too.

What makes Viking women different is that some of them are almost certainly professional warriors.

"Shield maidens" turn up in legend and saga, and archaeologists sometimes unearth the bones of women who were buried with weapons. Modern scholars point out that legend is … well … legend, and grave goods might just indicate status. However shield maidens will briefly charge across the pages of recorded history during the 10th century Siege of Dorostolon; in the aftermath of a raid, the Byzantines found female bodies amongst the fallen warriors.

There's also a clincher: a few centuries from now, the newly Christian Icelandic Vikings will enact laws forbidding women to wear men's clothing or use weapons. Why pass a law against shield maidens unless they exist?

What are shield maidens like?

Don't expect a chainmail bikini!

What with the layers of mail or padding, and the intimidating stature, you probably won't notice her gender as she stomps all over you – obviously, she's only going to be a warrior if she's good at it.

Beyond that, it's hard to tell you what to expect. The shield maidens in the sagas led normal warrior careers except that they happened to be female: they raided, fought, married, had children, got into feuds…

However, Viking legend also recounts shield maidens fighting as large military units, so we can wonder whether later Christianity has erased the memory of a cult of warrior priestesses. Scholars think that the Goddess Freyja may have been the chief of Odin's Valkyries. Perhaps her hall was originally the place where shield maidens went when they died…

Once the Viking era closes, women will have to wait another millennium before they are again welcome in the ranks of the military.

The same goes for other freedoms like divorce and owning property. Sure, 9th-century women's lives are perilous and exist in a legally enforced patriarchy, but that's true of all eras until very recently.

How come things are so relatively good? One glance at the history will tell you this is not a particularly nice era!

The answer is that it owes a lot to the roles women had to play.

Men needed wives who could deputise for them when they were away fighting, who could manage the household while the husband attended to the agriculture (because who else would you trust?), and who, as widows, would look after the interests of any surviving children. Women simply couldn't do all this without a good measure of legal and social freedom.

So, just as modern women owe much of their initial liberation to the demands of both World Wars, their Viking and Anglo-Saxon ancestors enjoy their freedoms thanks to the endless struggle of 9th-century life.

HALL AND HEARTH

Though England AD870 has what you would recognise as towns – especially London and Yorvic (York) – the bulk of the country is scattered with small settlements.

Sometimes, especially on the tougher-to-farm land, you'll find a single homestead struggling along. On the better land you'll find a hamlet of half a dozen families sharing a common ancestor. Sometimes there are proper villages sharing land or renting it from an overlord. And sometimes a lord's hall rises up like a massive upturned boat. The lord probably owns all the land you can see. If not he will be working on it. If you can see a nearby church, he's *probably* an Anglo Saxon *thegn*. If there's an oak tree with offerings hanging on it, he's a Viking *hersar* or even a *jarl*.

Though this is an island of farmers, don't think of the natives as primitives. They specialise in particular products, for example cheese, and trade at the local markets which used to happen at standalone "wics" but now – since the Vikings came – tend to take place in fortified burghs. You'll even find hi-tech watermills grinding out corn.

Though the churches tend to be of stone, everything else is timber-built, often to a high standard. Both Vikings and Anglo-Saxons are big on carpentry and wood carving.

Most settlements contain what archaeologists call "pit houses". When you see these, please dial home and let us know what they actually are!

The only traces pit houses leave behind are room-sized

145

holes in the ground with mark where a post supported the roof. They may actually be roofed over holes in the ground – perhaps weatherproof workshops or storage. However, the hole could equally well be a cellar with floorboards above.

Whatever they are, people don't live in pit houses. Early archaeologists found the pit houses easily, but missed the post holes left by the long rectangular above-ground houses where people actually lived. These are constructed by driving posts into the ground. The inside can be divided up using curtains or walls, with doors as convenient.

The largest houses are the halls belonging to lords with perhaps separate buildings for kitchen and bower, the women's quarters.

In the old days, nobody bothered with fortifications. Settlements crept across the landscape as old buildings well into disrepair and new ones rose. Now the householders, especially the rich ones, are keen on walls and gatehouses.

If you've watched old Robin Hood movies, you probably expect to find freedom-loving Anglo-Saxons with little or no class system. You may also have the idea that the Vikings exist in like wolves in a perpetual state of rough and ready barbarism.

Of course the truth is different. Both are organised into a pyramid. The slaves and thralls – increasingly unfree peasants – are at the bottom. However they're not the ones who you're likely to find yourself fighting shoulder to shoulder with, or going shield to shield against.

Above the rank of slave, society reflects military status since political power is very much military.

WARRIORS OF CLASS

If you encounter a mailed warrior with round shield, sensible helmet, spear and a sword in his belt, then he's probably a *hirdman*.

Have you noticed how modern main battle tanks all look a bit similar, regardless of the nation?

The same thing applies to the hirdman, the standard professional heavy infantryman of Earl Medieval Northern Europe.

Each hirdman belongs to a … you've guessed it … *hird*, the war band of a king or chieftain. This can be anything from fifty to perhaps three hundred men – more than that, and it's hard to ensure personal loyalty.

Hirdmen boast the best helmets, swords, and mail coats. Some of them may even find exotic import equipment like slashing spears and Byzantine-style lamellar armour.

There's probably more variation in the kit of Viking hirdmen because they are better travelled. Some Anglo-Saxon hirdmen meanwhile still use the single edged seax sword. Beyond that, the two cultures have different styles of ornaments on belt buckles and personal jewellery, but that's really as far as it goes.

All of them will carry a short *scramaseax*, a single edged knife, part utility blade, part combat dagger. Also, though they tend to fight on foot, a hirdman will have one or more horses for getting around on.

Where required, the king or chieftain equips his hirdmen by lending out weapons and armour. He also feasts them and loads them with treasure.

However, don't regard them as mercenaries.

If their lord falls in battle, hirdmen will fight to the death around his corpse. A hirdman without a lord laments his loneliness in a hostile world, not his empty purse.

It turns out that that treasure is really just a way of keeping score. There's not much to spend it on anyway, except perhaps followers: *A ring to adorn your sword as a badge of honour is worth more than a heap of gold coins.*

However, having to maintain a hird locks the kings and great chieftains into a cycle of violence. To maintain a hird, you need food and treasure. The best way to get these is through war, sometimes conquest but usually raiding; Lead your men to victory so that you can keep and expand your hird.

Of course, the snag is that you can't ever stop doing this because you need your hird to protect you and yours from the hirds of other great men. This is one reason why larger kingdoms are a good thing for the ordinary folk.

(**Housecarls**, *the famous Viking mercenaries, don't really exist yet. They belong to the 10th century and later. Hird-men, however, are probably not so dissimilar.*)

Though their hirdmen are almost interchangeable, the Anglo-Saxon and Viking kings sit on top of slightly different pyramids, especially in war-torn 9th century England.

ANGLO-SAXON WARRIORS

In later Medieval England, kings will fear their evil uncles, but in AD870 it is disgruntled nephews that they have to watch. The Anglo-Saxon kings are supposed to come from royal families. Son may follow father. However, but that depends on the Witan, the council of top nobles who tend to pick the best man for the job. If the late king's adult brother is a good leader, then he'll probably be chosen over an infant son. Unfortunately, children grow up fast.

Amongst the Anglo-Saxons, top ranking hirdmen are known as thegns.

A thegn can also be an important servant or administrator, but the ones we're interested in are like the infantry versions of Medieval knights; elite soldiers with their own followers.

Sooner or later the King grants them an estate – becoming a thegn has to be a hirdsman's retirement plan – and they join the ranks of the landed thegns. As long as they don't go broke or get killed, at least some of their sons will succeed them to that rank, and most of them will pass through a hird and become trained warriors.

Outside the King's hird, the rank of thegn is something that forces you to keep up a certain lifestyle. You need at least five hides of land – that's enough land to support five families – plus a church. You also need a home with a wall around it and a proper gate.

So thegns own farmland, but they are not farmers, they are lords.

This structure repeats with *ealdorman* – later to be known as *earls*. These are pretty much royal deputies appointed by the King to rule particular regions. Always drawn from the rich nobility and often of royal descent, an ealdormen has his own hird and can call on the service of local thegns.

Generally, when the King or an ealdorman calls out the army, this means summoning the "Select Fyrd", the thegns and their followers at one man per five hides. These are the warriors with the proper weapons and armour and the training to use it; spear, sword or axe, shield and helmet and mailcoat.

There will also be rich peasants – the coerls – who own that much land plus one lucky representative for each five hides of land in multiple ownership. Possibly the poorer coerls do duty as servants rather than fighters. However, they may also provide the specialist missile troops like slingers and bowmen, or logistic support with carts and boats.

When things go badly wrong, the King can call out the "Greater Fyrd", meaning all available freemen, including the coerls. This is a last resort because it means hazarding the farmers who produce the kingdom's wealth.

Greater Fyrd equipment is going to be a bit random and depend entirely one what farming folk have lying around their homes.

Because coerls are not rich, they will have neither expensive iron helmets nor mail coats. Because they are not warriors, they have made and maintained cheaper alternatives such as fabric armour and helmets of boiled leather. (Oh, and leather armour itself is not a cheap alternative – animal hide is expensive.)

Coerls are big on missile weapons such as bows and slings, since these have a civilian use. Similarly, most of them will have spears for hunting and home defence – spears are so common that poets refer to coerls as "ash bearers" (ash being the tree of choice for spear manufacture). There will be some shields of varying quality and vintage, perhaps smoke-stained from long years hanging on a wall and still chipped and battered from battle of yore.

The wealthier coerls will have axes and also scramaseaxes, those nasty choppy single edged knives. Everybody else will have clubs – which you shouldn't underrate; practically naked men with clubs have been known to take out entire units of heavily armoured cavalry.

Training? Not much unless a jarl or thegn has had time to muster the local fyrd, taught them to form a shield wall and walked them through some basic spear drill.

However, this doesn't make them useless in hand-to-hand combat. For a start, wrestling – which includes punches and kicks – is the pre-modern rural sport for young men, so much so that Medieval fencing masters will warn against rushing to grapple; *the peasant who can't use a sword can still throw you to the ground*. Add the scramaseax or club and you have a terrifyingly effective infighter.

On top of that, there's no reason why the Later Medieval peasant traditions of stick and quarterstaff fighting aren't already flourishing to provide grounding in club and spear.

So don't write off the ceorl. However, don't rely on him either. He isn't a hardened killer of men. Nor is he at home with the mayhem and madness of the battlefield.

Later in this century, King Alfred of Wessex will set up fortified "burghs", have the Select Fyrd rotate through as garrisons. The burghs will be rallying points and probably training camps for the Greater Fyrd. However, that will be his final response to the nemesis of the Anglo-Saxons, the Vikings…

VIKING WARRIORS

First, let's get this out of the way. NO BLOODY HORNED HELMETS.

There, better.

The Vikings have left us pictures of people with what *look* like horned helmets. However, the horns are actually stylised ravens and the wearer is Odin, God of War, or perhaps his priest. There's no trace of any such helmet in the archaeological record, no images of Viking warriors wearing them as standard issue, and no contemporary descriptions of warriors in horned helmets – the Anglo-Saxons are well aware that the Vikings are Heathen, so you'd expect them to make a fuss over something like that.

Anyway, it would be REALLY STUPID to go into close quarters combat with horns sticking out of the side of your helmet. They would get in your way when you fought, especially in a tight situation when you needed to whirl your sword or axe over your head. Worse, they would act as blade catchers, funnelling near misses and glancing blows to strike in just the wrong spot; *Horns? No thanks!*

Back home in Scandinavia, the Vikings have an increasingly structured society not so different from that of the Anglo-Saxons: kings and *jarls* (earls) rule *hersars* – local chieftains a lot like thegns – and all three have their own hirds. Together they rule over the farming classes, especially the *carls*, the free farmers. At the very bottom are the thralls, the slaves. Viking kings can also raise armies much like the Select Fyrd and the Greater Fyrd, though with more emphasis on ships.

So, everything is sewn up and the prospects for younger sons or ambitious minor nobles are poor. England, in contrast, is a land of opportunity.

Amongst the footloose Viking armies that rampage around the 9th century British isles, the ranking system appears to be based purely on capacity for organised violence.

You are a king if you have a large enough army to invade a kingdom rather than just raid it. You can be a king even if you share that army with several other kings.

You are a jarl (say it "yarl") if you could be a king, but obey one or more kings instead. Presumably you are a hersar if you have a band of followers and especially if you have some kind of ship.

(Once the Vikings start to settle, then you can add a territorial element. For example, Viking Dublin and Yorvic have no overlords, so are ruled by kings. Viking Orkney acknowledges Norwegian sovereignty, so is ruled by jarls.)

Obviously to go raiding, a Viking chieftain needs ships.

It follows that the first raiders were mostly hersars and jarls with their hirdmen bulked out by ambitious carls and maybe even thralls.

All ocean going Viking ships have big square sails. The hulls are "clinker built", meaning constructed of overlapping planks attached to each other so they can flex and squirm in rough seas. They have good solid keels, but fairly flat bottoms so they can skim through shallow water and land on beaches as required. You can also heave them onto rollers or a giant cart and haul them overland; this is how the Vikings get between rivers and lakes when crossing Russia, but it's also a great way of cutting across the long fingers of land separating the fjords of Scandinavia and the sea lochs of Scotland's west coast, especially if you're escaping superior forces.

There are, however, more than one kind of Viking ship.

The warships are usually called "longships" – they can be twenty or thirty metres long, so this is a good name. (They also tend to have carved dragons on their prows, so you can call them "dragonships" too.)

You can dismount the masts for battle and use oars for manoeuvring. Shields hang over the side – the salt water actually toughens up the leather facings – providing protection for the rowers. It's also a handy way of storing such bulky items. The rowers sit on their kit chests. Longships are specialist assault craft, wonderfully manoeuvrable but, having low sides, hard to handle in rough seas.

The smallest longship might have as few as forty oars, the largest – known as drakars or "dragons" – sixty. Don't take many more men than that on a long sea voyage. However, for an inshore naval battle you might just cram three times that number onto your dragon-prowed vessel.

Viking naval battles are not exactly glittering displays of tactics. They can't be. The ships don't have rams or artillery so they can't sink each other. It's all down to fiercely fought boarding actions. The way to win is to bracket one of their ships with two of yours. For this reason, when in doubt, Viking naval commanders lash the ships together to form massive floating fighting platforms.

Given that the ideal fighting crew is three times the ocean going crew, it's unlikely that all the Viking warriors travel by longship. Instead they'll go by cargo ship, still clinker built, but fat and stable with less chance of sinking and more capacity for loot.

This is a good thing because most Vikings aren't all expert sailors. For every great mariner able to judge his position by sniffing the wind and scrutinising the pattern of the waves, there's a multitude of comedy captains, always getting lost, being blown off course, and sinking. The 9th-century gold rush atmosphere must be bringing out the worst of them, judging from the way Viking fleets sink or get thrashed in battle; *Oh, and if anybody offers you a ride from Iceland to Greenland, say "no". The survival rate is just over 50%.*

However, in the late 9th century, most of the action is inland. For a minor Viking chieftain, having a ship is likely to be as much a liability as a benefit; *who will he trust to look after such an expensive item?*

The Vikings in England, AD870, are a mixture of professionals and amateurs, pirates and princes, outcasts and gentlemen amateurs. All this makes it hard to nail down what to expect in a Viking army.

The chieftains from king down to hersar will have mail coats or *lamellar* – eastern-style interlocking scaled armour. They'll certainly have iron helmets, some very fancy indeed with those cool spectacles to protect the eyes and perhaps a mask of ring mail hanging down beneath.

They'll also have fine swords, colourful shields, sturdy

spears, plus scramaseaxes for infighting and as general purpose knives.

Since the Vikings are freelance invaders, all the warriors following individual chieftains are technically hirdmen. However in this boom time, expect to find wild variation in equipment and training.

The core hirdmen of successful chieftains will be similarly equipped to their lords, if only from looted Anglo-Saxon equipment. However there will also be lesser folk on the make and thralls brought along as archers and slingers. Some of these will be lucky to have a helmet or shield. You may even see armour of padded reindeer hide brought from home.

There may also be very exotic warriors indeed.

Perhaps you'll encounter female fighters, individually, or in terrifying war bands devoted to a religious cult. You'll certainly meet professional berserks, warriors who work themselves up into an altered state of consciousness and prefer to fight naked or while wearing a wolf or bear skin.

The other kind of soldiers you'll encounter fighting for the Heathen Vikings are Christian Anglo-Saxons.

A Viking army is a great haven for any renegade warrior. However, in Northumberland and elsewhere, the Vikings have come as overlords. The surviving English aristocracy seem quite happy to join their armies to raid and invade; And why not? This is what Anglo-Saxons have always done.

This should be no surprise. Beyond religion, the Vikings and the Anglo-Saxons are not so very different and share common Germanic roots. Small wonder then that their approach to war is the same.

BATTLE

The swords of this era are pattern welded, carbon and iron braided and hammered together so that it seems a shimmering serpent dwells in the blade. A good sword has a name, is handed down from father to son, loaned by chiefs to favoured warriors. Use it right, God – or Odin – willing, and it will cleave shield and skull in a single blow and perhaps even shear through an iron helmet.

However, the sword is still a secondary weapon. Even great kings carry a spear into battle, sometimes in two hands. Typically, a warrior carries one spear for fighting, and several lighter ones – javelins–for throwing. Other weapons include axes and clubs – thrown or wielded– and a relatively cheap single-edged sword called a seax. You may find the odd warrior with an axe in two hands, though this weapon will have to wait a century or so before it truly flourishes.

There are also some exotic weapons. Slashing spears – technically a "glaive" – get talked about, but nobody now knows what they looked like. There's also something called an *angon*, the Early Medieval panzerfaust; a heavy spear with a barbed iron head on a really long neck. If it hits your mail, it goes through. If it hits your shield, it weighs it down and the iron neck stops you chopping it off. The thrower steps on the spear, tearing the shield from your grip and hits you with his sword.

If you find yourself wrestling for your life, there's always your knife, your trusty scramaseax.

You'll also find archers and cavalry.

The bows look like later longbows but are drawn to the chest. They'll penetrate ring mail at about 50m and wound an unarmoured man at double that distance. Enough men and enough arrows and you can work up a respectable arrow storm.

The cavalry ... this is something modern historians still argue over. Vikings certainly grab horses when they can, and there are saga descriptions of Viking-on-Viking cavalry duels. The English were big on horse breeding, so it would seem odd if they never rode horses into battle. If you believe the saga description of the Battle of Stamford Bridge in 1066, the English can field swarms of javelin-armed cavalry when they want to.

However, in this world, bowmen are not really decisive except as snipers, and cavalry are reduced to scouting, skirmishing and pursuit. This is because this is the age of the shieldwall.

The shields of this era are about 60cm across, round and made of criss-crossed layers of wood and ox hide. A metal boss in the middle protects the hand grip. The cheaper shields have conical bosses made of rolled sheets of iron, the more expensive ones sport something properly dished and even tempered. If your shield gets hacked up, you can fight on using the boss as a buckler.

The point about these shields is that you stand shoulder-to-shoulder with your brothers in arms to make up a shieldwall. It is this that will enable you to weather the arrowstorm and taunt the cavalry as they mill around your front.

This is a heroic age, but battles are very much a collective effort: American football with more weapons and less protective clothing. Though battles can be clever, with feigned retreats, outflanking actions, lines extending and enveloping, the default probably looks like this...

The two sides shake themselves out into shield walls, perhaps three or four men deep, swords and axes at the front, spears at the back.

Once they can truly see each other, both sides pause to psyche themselves up.

In the old days, this was the moment when warriors would trade insults, fight duels. You might also see: Heathen spear dancers; men raising their shields as primitive megaphones and chanting their battle cry; and long haired warriors going out front and head banging as if they were at a Heavy Metal gig.

However the archers and slingers quickly fill the air with missiles. The men with the better bows turn sniper – it's not a safe thing to be a chieftain or to stand near one unless the hirdmen are on the ball.

At last both sides let out a rising battle cry and surge forward. The shieldwalls clash with a noise that startles the crows a mile away. For a moment the men in the front are crushed against their own shields while the spears of the second rank go in over their shoulders. Now is a good moment for the back ranks to chuck javelins or clubs.

If one side breaks, then the other simply tramples anybody who falls over and moves to pursuing them – we'll come to that.

Otherwise the sides blur together as men fall dying and enemy warriors shoulder in to widen the gap by hacking down the men on either side.

Now is the moment for champions with swords and good mail coats. The men behind them blunder in over the fresh corpses, and perhaps the enemy line breaks –

– or perhaps all those big shields and thrusting points shove back the intruders leaving some of them dead and the others bleeding and exhausted. If so, the shieldwalls recoil, dress the lines, work themselves up to repeat the process.

Sometimes this phase goes differently and one side – perhaps the outnumbered one – adopts the ancient "boar's snout formation", basically a crude wedge with two ambitious and possibly foolhardy warriors forming the point.

Boar's snouts seem to work by approaching the enemy line, chucking all the available javelins at one spot, then charging home with an almighty roar.

If you are crazy enough to be leading the wedge, then you have five or six men behind you shoving you onward. However, if the shields are properly locked, then some of the force of the rest of the wedge is coming to bear on your back. Don't worry, the pressure won't last long.

Unless it is very deep indeed, an opposing shield wall simply can't withstand the collision. It just has to split. The boar's snout can now break in two and outflank each half of the enemy line from the middle.

The counter to this is for the defenders to fall back to form a receiving V shape to accept the boar's snout. Well-led hirdmen should be able to pull this off, but it must take a lot of courage to manoeuvre in the face of a howling mob of enemy bearing down on you.

If the combatants don't withdraw from each other, sooner or later, the battle devolves into a chaotic melee, with men feeling for good footing between the piles of corpses.

Melees like this seem to last forever, but take less than a few minutes. They are a fleeting chance for the individual warrior to prove himself, and for chiefs to show they still have what it takes.

Almost anything can happen. While you battle a mighty champion, shield-to-shield, a ceorl or churl three metres away can drive a long spear through your throat, or a sharp eyed archer can shoot you in the throat from far away.

The almost insane randomness of the melee makes it the place where larger sides lose battles they should have won, and smaller sides snatch a victory by killing the enemy chieftain.

However, often as not, the melee ends with both sides

pulling back to regroup. They dress their ranks, realise how many friends are missing, and stand with shaking limbs, paying the price for the adrenalin-fuelled violence. After a while they may muster up the courage to continue the battle. However they are just as likely to withdraw; *Enough for one day.*

If, however, during the melee, one side does melt away – leaving the hirdmen to die fighting over their fallen chief–then the battle becomes a pursuit.

As modern psychologists will tell you, it's psychologically hard to kill a man face-to-face. It would be nice to think it was because humans have an aversion to murder. However the sad truth is that the inhibitions magically drop away when the enemy is fleeing.

Now is the time for the lightly armed folk to pick up spears and sprint after the warriors who could so easily kill them if they stood their ground, and for anybody with a horse to mount and join the hunt.

The snag with the pursuit is that a well-led foe can suddenly rally and turn on the disorganised pursuers, defeating them as they arrive in dribs and drabs.

This fear of being caught out is probably one of the reasons why the the end game is usually less bloody than battles in other eras. Also, the armies are too small to have large cavalry wings, and the bulk of the warriors are tired and want to attend to wounded comrades.

There's also the circumstances of the battle to consider. The smaller side usually has fortifications it can withdraw into if it loses, and dare not risk pursuing the larger side if it wins. And Vikings can usually flee to their ships, Anglo-Saxons to their burghs, both sides to their horses.

Nobody really knows the casualty rate for Viking era battles. Looking at better-recorded High Medieval battles, it would not be a surprise to find each side taking around

10% casualties in the clash and melee, then the losing side taking another 10% as it ran away – more if cavalry or angry peasants were present.

One thing is certain, the casualties are rarely crippling. You can thrash an army one month, only to have to flee from it the next.

This, plus the ready supply of Viking re-enforcements, is probably why the Viking wars went on so long.

THE VIKING WARS

And so it begins...

England, Kingdom of Wessex, AD789 or thereabouts.

Three ships run up the beach and disgorge a party of Scandinavians.

The local reeve, one Beaduheard, rides out to greet them; *Wessex welcomes traders from afar. Please come with me to the royal estate.*

This was business as usual for the reeve. Did he notice something different? Do the visitors' smiles not quite reach their cold blue eyes? Do the ships seem rather … empty of trade goods?

Older books make this into a first contact situation: a dragon-prowed vessel drawn up on the beach, furry-legged barbarians with Thor's Hammer amulets and horned helmets bemused by the little Christian bureaucrat.

But that can't be how it was.

No horned helmets, for a start – *but you knew that!* – and the Scandinavians won't have looked so different from the English with whom they shared ancestors. Probably no dragon-prowed longships either, otherwise the reeve would have not have mistaken them for merchants.

Nor can they have been aliens. Scandinavians had plied the North Sea since Roman times, and they turn up all over Europe as merchants, mercenaries, and of course, raiders. It's also clear from what happened next that these visitors knew their way around England…

So the reeve orders the Scandinavians to report to the manor house.

And the Scandinavians do go to the manor, but only to ransack it after murdering the poor reeve.

Because these aren't ordinary Scandinavians, they're Vikings! (Not that anybody called them that very often. In the old chronicles, they're usually interchangeably "Northmen" or "Danes".)

Loaded with booty, the Vikings hurry back to the beach, past the corpse of the reeve, throw everything into the ships and shove them back into the sea. Striped sails billowing in the wind, they skip away through the waves and are gone.

If help arrives, it finds only a burning manor house, corpses, and skid marks in the sand.

That's the thing about Vikings; they can hit the coast anywhere they can find a shallow beach or a river mouth, wreak havoc, grab their loot and leg it before the locals concentrate their forces.

Spare a tear for Beaduheard the Reeve (deceased), but don't feel too sorry for the main victims. The only non-Churchmen with anything worth stealing are the nobility, and for them raiding is a way of life.

More than just a hobby, raiding is how kings and nobles show who's top dog. It's also the best way to build up your hird, the private army you need to protect your property from raiders!

No, the problem with the Vikings isn't a moral one, it's a technical one. What do you do when it's almost impossible to catch the raiders in the act, and actually impossible to mount any sort of counter raid?

Elderly King Offa of Mercia responds by organising defences against "pagan seamen". No doubt other kings do the same. But it's not possible to cover every stretch of coastline.

In AD793, Viking vessels turn into a small river mouth on the island of Lindisfarne of the coast of Northumberland, and pull up on the shore next to Lindisfarne Abbey.

Back in AD547, that sheltered river mouth is probably what brought Theoderic and his Heathen Angles to the island. Now, however, the island is best known for the monastery founded a century later by St Aidan, an Irish monk. Irish monks have a tradition of "desert places" away from the rest of humanity, and island has the added bonus of giving your missionaries easy access to the "ship roads."

Of course, it also gives the ship roads access to your monastery.

Lindisfarne Abbey began as a humble base for Christianising Northern England. However, on the day the Vikings arrive, it's crammed with two centuries' of pious gifts, plus the profits from its Bible factory.

The Vikings don't care much about piety, they do care about all that lovely loot. And so they sack Lindisfarne Abbey.

They also – say the chronicles – slaughter the monks.

This isn't some kind of pagan backlash. These Vikings aren't "Crusaders for Odin". Possibly that kind of thing went on in Northern France when the Danes and the Carolingian Franks butted heads. However, judging from what came before, and what's going to happen, the Vikings pursue just one goal systematically; *steal other people's stuff.*

Why then do they cut down so many monks? Alas, this is just how warriors behave. This kind of things still goes on in modern times and gets investigated by the UN.

When wild fighting men break into a place they rampage around wrecking things and killing anybody they find. It's probably hard-wired from times when bands of pre-humans made the most of any chance to eliminate each other. Even more modern armies will have a hard time preventing it – ask the Duke of Wellington. This day in the Early Middle Ages, the Vikings aren't even trying to dial back the carnage.

So this is not a good time to be in Lindisfarne Abbey.

But are the monks *really* just standing – or kneeling – around while the Vikings scythe them down?

Probably not.

For a start they have the option to flee into the island's interior. It's not a big island, but the Vikings are here to steal things. Are they really going to spend the day blundering around sheepfolds and sand dunes looking for monks to kill?

Most likely, though, the monks that get killed are those that stand their ground.

At minimum, some are following the grand tradition of seeking martyrdom and a free pass to Heaven. The Vikings are already a bit nervous because they're violating a religious sanctuary. Now they're confronted by oddly-dressed fanatics chanting in unfamiliar tongues; *By Thor! A hostile magician! Quick, Olaf, get him with your spear!*

Or perhaps, the Lindisfarne monks who get killed are the ones who fight back. Monks are on record defending their monasteries in Dark Age Europe, and in the next century, Irish monks will take up arms against the Vikings. These Lindisfarne monks probably come from noble families and have at least some martial training. They're also sitting on a massive trove of treasure. Why wouldn't they put up a fight?

Oddly, historians don't seems to have considered this

option. Perhaps we've all bought into the Medieval Church's PR: monasteries as spiritual power houses inhabited by mild mannered men of special piety.

Some people really did live up to this ideal. However, compared to the rough-tough Early Medieval life, monasteries were rather nice places to live, especially if you were a landless younger son of a noble family.

And monasteries themselves were land hungry – English kings kept having to confiscate land in order to reward their warriors! – and they were implacable landlords, living off the work of the peasants. How socially useful monasteries were depends on whether you think their prayers were effective. They certainly didn't keep off the Vikings…

Finally, though, there's a strong possibility that not all the monks who went missing actually died. The Vikings were great slave traders, and a monastery is a fantastic place to find a whole load of highly marketable educated young men. Why young men? To serve the Greek and Persian market for eunuchs: *The good news, young Anglo-Saxon, is that you're going to go and live in a palace where you will be surrounded by pretty girls. The bad news…*

So, now the Vikings are here and there, and everywhere – Look for the smoke! – knocking over monasteries and settlements, knocking down anybody in their way.

Sometimes the Vikings hit coastal places. Sometimes they go up river in their shallow-draughted boats and strike inland. Sometimes they steal horses and pillage a zigzag course through England's heartland.

The Viking Age has started, and it won't really stop until the descendants of Vikings crush the last Anglo-Saxon king at the Battle of Hastings in AD1066.

WHERE DID THE VIKINGS COME FROM?

Where did these Vikings come from? Why were there so many of them?

An old argument is that the Vikings came because they now could, thanks to recent developments in ship technology; that clinker building techniques and sturdy keels enabled them for the first time to weather the North Sea.

This doesn't wash because Northern raiders had crossed the sea before in the 4th century and made such pests of themselves that the Romans referred to the "Saxon Shore" and set up a line of forts to defend it.

Another argument is that Vikings started to raid England because they had been rebuffed from France. This is possibly true, but it just pushes the problem back further. Raiding itself wasn't new – Beowulf's uncle got himself killed doing just that back in AD516. Why did the Vikings start raiding France, and then England so vigorously?

This takes us to the two most likely explanations.

First, there may have been more footloose Viking young men knocking around than before. Take your pick for why. Did switching agriculture to cattle make for a high protein diet, ensuring more children survived into young adulthood and grew bigger and meaner? Or did changes to inheritance customs mean that the younger sons had to fend for themselves? Or had they run out of land? Of did they practice female infanticide?

Second, blame the victims. By the end of the 8th century, France and England had well-organised administrations, rich monasteries and churches, and an economy – or at least a tax system–based on money. Rich pickings for Viking raiders.

It gets worse...

The raiding continues for the next generation; just a monastery plundered here, a coastal settlement there. The

English kings can't feel very threatened. However, they should. The Vikings have been busy grabbing the islands around the British coast, the Orkneys, the Shetlands, the Hebrides, the Isle of Man, and starting to nibble at Ireland.

Where we see water, the Vikings see a freeway – the shiproad – giving them easy access to the mainland. To them, a well-placed island is like a handy mother ship or an aircraft carrier, a place to overwinter until the next raiding season.

Meanwhile, it's business as usual in England. The Northumbrians fight a civil war. Their northern border secure, the Mercians gobble up the East Saxons, Kent and East Anglia, lay waste to the Welsh Kingdom of Dyfed and conquer neighbouring Powys. King Ecgberht of Wessex runs counter insurgency operations in Cornwall, and pursues a cold war with Mercia by encouraging the East Anglian independence movement. The cold war becomes a hot war, King Ecgberht conquers Mercia, installs a puppet king, ravages Northumberland into submission and starts on the Welsh.

You could say that King Ecgberht of Wessex is consolidating, forging a nation, preparing England to meet its destiny. However, King Offa of Mercia did just the same a generation ago, and since the Anglo-Saxons came to England, just about every kingdom has had a turn including Northumberland, Kent, and plucky little East Anglia. It's what English kings do. They fight for power and glory, not principle or morality, and they leave behind legends, not legacies.

So now, in AD835, King Ecgberht of Wessex is top dog of England, Bretwalda as they call it – and that's when the Vikings materialise a massive fleet and land on him like a metric tonne of bricks.

First they rampage up the English Channel, ravaging

town and country on both sides. As always they are hard to catch, but King Ecgberht does catch them the following year at Carhampton in Somerset.

Carhampton has a Royal Estate. Perhaps the Vikings targeted it, and the king happened to be there, or perhaps he was using it as a base and got lucky. The Vikings have thirty five shiploads of warriors, something like between one thousand and two thousand men. King Ecberht, probably has at least same numbers or he would not have chosen to fight. However it's hard to keep an army in the field, plus Wessex has too many military commitments. So King Ecberht is probably leading his own hird plus the local Greater Fyrd.

The Vikings slaughter them.

A couple of years later, the Vikings abandon hit and run and gang up with the Cornish, the oppressed Celtic people on the toe of Wessex. This is the kind of warfare the Anglo-Saxons are good at, and King Ecberht defeats them. A year later he's dead and his sons divide his kingdom.

After this, it's mostly down to local defence with English Ealdormen winning about half their battles against Vikings raiders. Given that the Vikings plunder London, Rochester and Southampton, we have to wonder what a victory really means – remember when the going gets tough, the Vikings can just hop in their ships and get going.

AD850, and Ealdorman Ceorl leads the men of Devon to victory over the Vikings. However, the Vikings decide to overwinter on Thanet, the little island on the South East corner of England. The English are losing.

The next year, 350 Viking ships sail up the Thames and pillage London and Canterbury.

The same pattern continues, except on a grander scale. The English keep claiming victories over the Vikings, but more – or the same Vikings – pop up again. The ones that raided Southampton in 842 were fresh from ravaging France, so there were plenty of new Vikings ready to take the place of the fallen ones.

But, how many Vikings did fall in their defeats? The battles of this era rarely end in wholesale slaughter; it's too hard to catch a fleeing enemy. Moreover, the Vikings are here to steal, not to take and hold ground. Faced by an army, why not just conduct a fighting withdrawal, leaving the English with the field and a technical claim to victory? Even if the Vikings do stand and fight, then suffer a defeat, they can retreat to their ships and avoid being massacred. So the Viking problem is not going to go away anytime soon.

This doesn't seem to bother the English kings. They squabble with their families, tinker with the coinage, gang up on the Welsh, and in one case go on pilgrimage to Rome. Perhaps they've got used to hammering down Viking incursions. Ten years pass like this.

Then in AD864, the Vikings in Thanet make peace with the men of Kent, and everything changes; raiders don't make peace with the locals, invaders do.

Worse, these invaders are led by a slippery character who is like a cross between Erwin Rommel and Vlad the Impaler; King Ivar the Boneless.

MEET IVAR THE BONELESS...

Like a piranhas under the surface of English history, the Vikings have been busy swarming in the Irish Sea. It's not clear when they founded Dublin on the east coast of Ireland – the name just means "long port". What started as a base for raiding and trading what was raided, like any barracks town now, now has its shops and taverns.

The Irish kings would prefer to ally with the Vikings than resist them. Ireland is a lot like the Scandinavia a hundred or so years before. There are LOTS of Irish kings, at least 150 of them jostling and stepping on each other in order to get to the top of the pile.

By the AD840s, the Viking kings of Dublin are already halfway to becoming Irish, taking sides in local conflicts, making treaties. They even team up with Irish kings to knock over the odd monastery. However, when the Vikings try to extend their rule inland, the Irish kings combine and give them a good thrashing.

That's in AD848. In the same year, other Vikings sense weakness and the claim jumpers start to turn up.

The Irish call these newcomers the "Dark Foreigners", and they call the local Vikings, the "Fair Foreigners". The first is a chieftain called Thorir who gets himself killed in battle somewhere near Dublin. Then in AD851 another wave of Vikings turn up and attack the first lot. They're from "Laithlind", which could be a Norwegian kingdom, or could be the Scottish Islands. Or could be some kind of joke; the literal translation is "Mud Pool".

The details are hazy, but it looks as if they're led by a Viking known to legend as Ivar the Boneless. In case you haven't taken the hint, he's a man to watch.

WHY "THE BONELESS"?

A 13th-century saga tells us that a prophetess warned Ragnar Lodbrok, Ivar's father, not to consummate his marriage on his wedding night. Being a lusty Viking, Ragnar ignored this advice. The resulting son, Ivar, was born without bones.

According to the same saga, this somewhat Lovecraftian fate didn't stop Ivar from becoming King of all England

and Ireland. His tomb was said to guard England from future invasion. It apparently worked because King Harald Hardrada was killed nearby.

The saga also tells us that Ragnar Lodbrok himself…

…came to the throne of Denmark at an early age, saw off rival claimants, conquered swathes of the known world, married a shield maiden, divorced her, wore furry trousers as anti-venom protection in order to slay two serpents – hence the nickname; Lodbrok means "hairy breeches", which in turn won him the daughter of the King of Sweden…

By now you've realised that this version of Ivar the Boneless and his dad are as fictitious as the British Arthur and Uther Pendragon; a mishmash of real men of similar name, and deeds taken from folklore and poet's fantasy.

Viking sagas give us stirring stories that are rich in detail. However, sagas are mostly written two centuries after the events they describe, and it's never clear how much of any given saga is just historical fiction. It's like – say – trying to work out what happened in World War Two using only 20th century war films!

The only sources we can (mostly) trust are the English and Irish chronicles written near the time, dry lists of names, events and dates. They're trustworthy, but dull.

However, there's one Viking story about Ivar and Ragnar that you might choose to believe.

King Aelle of Northumberland captured Ragnar and threw him into a pit of vipers to die. When Ivar caught up with King Aelle, he carved a "blood eagle" on his back: hacked open his ribcage on either side of his spine and – while Aelle still lived – pulled out his lungs so they flapped like wings. (We'll get to King Aelle.)

As for "Boneless"?

Could be sexual dysfunction, but he appears to have

sired a dynasty. Could be that he was disabled in some way, but it's hard to see how he could have thrived as a Viking. Could be an ironic name, like the English "Little John; perhaps he was big and virile. Me? I think he was one of those wiry buggers who's hard to hit with a spear because he can just writhe his body out of the way.

So, Ivar the Boneless storms Dublin and slaughters the defenders. He does the same at Linns. The next year there's a showdown at Carlingford Loch, and Ivar and his Dark Foreigners triumph. Ivar is now King Ivar.

Then something odd happens.

In AD853, Olaf the White sails in from Laithlind – wherever that is – and everybody submits to him.

Olaf the White is, probably, Ivar's brother. Is he yet another claim jumper? *"Move over squirt, big brother is here!"* Perhaps "Boneless" means "spineless". This won't be the last time Ivar lets a brother take over.

However, legend makes King Ivar the wise leader of a band of terrifying brothers. We really only know dates, events and names, but let's assume that's how it was; *By Thor, brother Olaf! You took your time!*

So, King Ivar the Boneless, Olaf the White and a third brother, Asl, spend a decade fighting to consolidate their conquests in Ireland.

They have to take on the Foreigner-Gaels – think "super warriors created when the Vikings and the Irish fought to a standstill and the survivors bred". Both sides have Irish allies, Olaf even marries a local princess – *Beauty and the Beast,* but with more axes and bloodshed.

It all ends when Olaf drowns one King Conchobar in church font, leaving their ally King Lorcan as the local big man. The fighting isn't over, but the Dark Foreigners are established.

Olaf the White sails off to attack Dumbarton, the gateway to the Scottish mainland. King Ivar the Boneless decides to turn claim jumper and heads for England with a large army.

IVAR IN ENGLAND

So the army making peace with the people of Kent is led by Ivar the Boneless. The English chronicles don't take much notice of the leadership but, impressed by its sheer size, call it the "Great Army".

Once again there's a younger brother around, a Viking called Halfdan.

His base secured, Ivar hops over into East Anglia and the East Anglians make peace with him; *Here, take our horses, please. (Perhaps you'll ride away and stop bothering us.)*

Ivar is making peace in order to prepare for war. But where does he strike next?

Ivar the Boneless could strike for London. He could plunge deep into Wessex and loot the towns and estates of its heartland – it's been done before, and will be done again. Instead he blitzes 200 miles inland to York; *Those East Anglian horses have come in useful.*

Anglo-Saxon York is called Eoforwic, "Boar Town". It's almost a double town, split by the River Ouse. On the south bank rise the old Roman walls of what was once Eboricam – Roman-British, "Yew Tree Town". These now enclose a merchant settlement. There'll be the houses of local traders and hospitality to be had for a price.

Opposite, on the north shore, there's the old Legionary Fort with intact walls and even the original great hall from the Headquarters building. There's a palace, a cathedral, a school and a library. This is the place that launched the saintly Alcuin on his career as adviser to Emperor Charlemagne. It's more than a royal centre, it's a cultural hub.

Unfortunately, there's nobody home, or at least neither of the two kings currently competing for the crown. There's a civil war going on.

York is part of the Kingdom of Northumberland. This takes in not just Northumberland, but also modern Yorkshire and stretches from the River Humber up into what's now Scotland, ending at the Firth of Forth.

Northumberland's kings may no longer be *Bretwaldas*, but it is a rich, powerful and cultured Kingdom. Unfortunately, it's also beset by civil war. King Osberht, of royal descent, has been displaced by Aelle, who is probably not. It's the same old story of inept king and over-mighty subject. Both men have armies, so this is going to go on for more than one campaigning season. And while these kings are destroying their kingdom to show how much they love it, they are not paying much attention to the outside world…

…and here's the lovely city of Eoforwic – modern York – wealthy, strategically located, and ripe for a name change.

So King Osberht and King Aelle are elsewhere, engaged in competitive peasant slaying. King Ivar and Great Army Vikings thunder into town. In just a blink of an eye Eoforwic has become Yorvic, "Horse Bay", which seems appropriate, since Ivar's strike force arrives on horses.

At this point, the Northumbrian chronicles abruptly cease. Nobody's writing them. The monks are either dead, or on their way East to feed the eunuch trade.

Once again, the Vikings bring about peace, but this time between the warring kings. King Osberht and King Aelle spend the winter sorting themselves out, making deals, then combine forces and attack Yorvic.

The Northumbrians kings mount an epic assault. They hack their way through the old Roman defences – which side of the river isn't clear. However, once inside, things go badly wrong. Both kings die in the street fighting – unless you believe the Blood Eagle story – and with them fall eight ealdorman.

The surviving Northumbrians make peace. Victorious Ivar then puts one Egbert, a native, on the throne of the northern part of Northumberland, the old Anglian Kingdom of Bernicia and at least one churchman is left alive to become archbishop.

What's going on?

It's possible that it was Egbert who brought in the Great Army, only to discover it was a spectacularly bad idea. It's also possible that Ivar the Boneless and his Viking comrades have no desire to blunder about the mountains and wastes of Northumberland hunting Englishmen; *They don't want land, they want a kingdom.*

The next year, in AD 867, King Ivar strikes south into Mercia and winter in Nottingham (originally, *Snotingham*, "The People of Snot's Village", but – please! – let's use the modern spelling).

King Burgred of Mercia calls in his brother-in-law, King Ethelred of Wessex. However, the canny Ivar refuses to have it out in an epic battle and King Burgred decides it's easier to buy him off; *Vikings, here's some money, now go home.*

This works against raiders. Not so against invaders.

Ivar the Boneless leads the Great Army home to Yorvic. They sit there for a year, consolidating, carousing, being cruel (apparently). Then, in AD869, Ivar thrusts south again. This time he passes through neutral Mercia and hits East Anglia, the kingdom connecting Mercia to his subject kingdom of Essex.

We've seen the Vikings make peace. Now watch them make a saint.

Ivar's hardened veterans make short work of the East Anglian army. Judging from the lack of East Anglian chronicles, they probably also loot most of the local monasteries.

Meanwhile, Ivar tries to repeat what he's done in Northumberland, and leave a native under king in charge.

Inconveniently, East Anglia is ruled by a saintly virgin, one King Edmund, who refuses to submit to Heathens. Ivar has him beaten, tied to a tree and used for archery practice. When that doesn't work, he has him beheaded. The royal head rolls under a bush, where it attracts a howling wolf (or a grieving hunting dog). Superstitious Vikings permit a hasty Christian burial in a makeshift chapel. The chapel quickly becomes a place of miraculous healing, and the ineffective Edmund, a saint.

So, King Ivar has bounced around England like a pinball, but with more purpose. Ivar has two solid blocks of territory: Northumberland and the South East of England, with neutral Mercia as a corridor between them.

He now leaves it to brother Halfdan to finish the job and heads back to Yorvic.

Ivar the Boneless pushes north from Yorvic and joins forces with Olaf the White for a second go at Dumbarton.

Dumbarton is the ultimate natural castle. The site is so good that it looks as if some kid made it in Minecraft: a shear volcanic rock with a sloping cleft leading to the summit. Stick a short wall across the cleft and you have a castle.

Dumbarton is also the capital of Strathclyde, the last British kingdom to survive outside Wales. It's outlasted the Roman occupation, and weathered the early Dark Ages when the Scots came from Ireland and the Anglians from Denmark. Olaf and King Ivar, however, storm it. The Viking brothers commit the kind of acts that would these days interest UN observers, and decamp to Ireland laden with booty and slaves.

The next year, Olaf the White goes rampaging in Pictland and the Picts kill him.

Ivar the Boneless lives on until AD873 and then dies in his bed leaving his son Barid to become King of Dublin.

In noting death, the Irish chronicles call Ivar "King of Northmen of all Ireland and Britain". They also comment that his death welcomes in a forty year peace.

(By the way some modern academics reckon King Ivar the Boneless didn't really exist, and that there were at least two Ivars. The reasoning is that the Viking sagas say Irish Ivar is Norwegian, and the English chronicles and some other sagas make their Ivar out to be Danish!)

However, the sagas were pretty obviously making stuff up to fit stories together; *General Patton's cool, let's make him Winston Churchill's long lost son by his first marriage with Queen Victoria!*

Meanwhile, to the contemporary English chroniclers, anybody with a Scandinavian accent and a bad attitude was a "Dane" or "Norwegian", sometimes in the same sentence.

Also, it would be really, really odd if Irish Ivar decided to stay home and rest for precisely the years that English Ivar was storming around Northumberland and East Anglia, and then if English Ivar quietly dropped dead just before Irish Ivar overcame his malaise and decided to storm Dumbarton.

HALFDAN vs ALFRED

So back in England, AD870, what will Halfdan conquer next? Wales, worth invading only if you enjoy being ambushed in a mountain pass? Or lovely fertile rolling Wessex, the rich kingdom that makes up the foot and toe of England?

Wessex it is, then.

Of course, the snag with Wessex is that what makes it attractive must also make it hard to conquer. Being rich means its warriors are well-equipped, its defences prepared. Being rich also means that it has been a target for generations. Given it has survived, its military traditions must be well honed, and its soldiers, veterans. If Wessex doesn't quite have the habit of victory, it has at least proven itself a survivor.

More importantly, Wessex is sophisticated for its time. Its rulers are much more like medieval monarchs than mere barbarian warlords good at murdering rivals and splitting skulls. One of them, the under-king, is Alfred, known to History (SPOILER ALERT) as "Alfred the Great".

Meanwhile, with scary Ivar the Boneless out of the way, it's not clear that King Halfdan is really in full control of the Vikings Great Army. Really it's a coalition of bearded gangsters. Since "King" just means "top dog", then if Halfdan is a king, so is a certain Bagsecg. There are also a mess of self-styled jarls, lesser war lords, all keen to get to the top, or else get rich trying.

The resulting invasion looks a little shambolic.

The Great Army ride inland. They brush aside a local force and grab Reading, handily placed in defensible angle between the Thames and the River Kennet.

Two jarls impatiently charge off in search of loot.

The local ealdorman, Ethelwulf pounces on them, routs them, slays one of the jarls.

By this time, King Ethelred and kid brother Alfred have gathered their main army.

They swoop on Reading and slaughter any Vikings they catch outside its walls. However, in the resulting confusion, the Vikings sally out of their defences and rout the English. Poor Ealdorman Ethelwulf is one of those slain.

Ethelred and Alfred rally their men at Ashdown, a long chalk ridge. Asser, Alfred's pocket Welsh monk has given us a detailed account of the battle. However, being a priest, he's focused on the piety of Edgar, the inspired bravery of Alfred, and not on tactics. Here's what seems to happen:

King Halfdan turns up with his Great Army, grabs the higher ground and there's a face off. Both armies create field fortifications. Only a lunatic would attack fortifications without overwhelming superiority. At this point people usually pay off the Vikings and everybody goes home. Instead, the West Saxons draw themselves up for battle.

These are both big armies, so large that each can only handle command and control by splitting into two.

King Halfdan and King Bagsecg take one half the Viking army so they can keep an eye on each other, and a mob of jarls take the other half.

Meanwhile, each of the royal West Saxon brothers takes a half of their army. (According to Asser, Alfred will attack the jarls while Edgard handles the "Heathen Kings", though it's not clear how this worked out in practice.)

Alfred advances and his men start skirmishing – shooting into the fort or hurling rocks.

It's a trap and the Viking jarls fall for it. Breaking discipline, the jarls lead their men out of their fortifications. The Viking front slams into Alfred's tightly packed shield wall.

For a fleeting moment, half the Viking army is exposed outside its fortifications, possibly the most amateur half. Worse still, they are outnumbered two to one and disorganised by their charge.

Edgar hurries up, smashes into the Viking flank and starts chomping through the invaders. The Viking jarls lead from the front, but in the press this doesn't make much difference. Pretty soon most of them are cut down

– Sidroc the Old, Sidroc the Younger, Osbearn, Fræna and Harold – Viking chiefs who will trouble the Anglo-Saxons no more.

King Halfdan and King Bagsecg can't afford to lose half the army, and neither dare look like a coward, so they lead their force to the rescue.

However, it's no longer an even fight. The jarls' force has been thoroughly mauled. Since it must exit its own defences, the Viking kings' force can only arrive piecemeal. The men of Wessex, meanwhile, are flushed with victory. King Bagsecg falls – *or does Halfdan stab him in the back?* – and soon the surviving Vikings are conducting a fighting retreat into the night. The exhausted West Saxons let them go.

This is a massive victory for King Edgar and Alfred.

However, it's not a total disaster for King Halfdan. He still has an army, he can always find more footloose Vikings to replace the fallen. Better yet, Bagsecg and most of the troublesome jarls are slain.

Now King Halfdan strikes back. With an undivided command, victory comes easily, first at Basing and then at Meretun where the West Saxons rout the Vikings, who then rally and defeat the now-disorganised natives.

Better still, success breeds success and a Summer Army of Vikings sails up the Thames to join Halfdan at Reading. It's led by a chieftain called Guthrum – keep an eye on him.

Reinforced, in sole command of his army, what could go wrong for King Halfdan?

Some time after Easter, AD 871, King Etheldred of Wessex dies. Alfred is now King of Wessex.

Alfred is an interesting character. He's every bit the Old Germanic warrior king, leading from the front, smiting away in the midst of the mayhem. However, he's also clever. It's more obvious in later life when he not only learns Latin and translates ancient texts into English but also re-organises the defences of Wessex pretty much the way a modern strategy gamer would.

So when you read about Alfred the Great, think "Alfred the Geek".

So now it's King Halfdan versus King Alfred.

Alfred, now with a stripped down force – presumably he sent home the Greater Fyrd – takes on King Halfdan in Wilton and gets beaten.

After that it gets blurry. All in all, AD871 sees something like two dozen battles. The West Saxons "lose" most of them, but this doesn't seem to matter. What's going on?

Alfred is on his home ground. There's always somewhere fortified to retreat to. The wealthier West Saxon soldiers fight as infantry, but probably have horses on which to escape. So being defeated merely means leaving the field to the Vikings. A tactical victory doesn't always imply a strategic – *big picture* – victory. This is the kind of warfare Von Clausewitz will write about nearly a thousand years later. The only way of securing a strategic victory is to destroy the enemy army, and that's obviously very hard to do.

As winter approaches, King Halfdan and King Alfred "make peace". The Vikings retire to winter quarters in London. (Halfdan even acts like a real king and issues coins in his own name.)

Both sides probably expect more fighting in the spring. However, at this point the Northumbrians rebel and expel King Ecberht, the puppet king Ivar the Boneless installed after the final battle of Yorvic.

King Halfdan leads his army north, spends a year putting down the rebellion and winters in Northumberland.

It's now AD873 and it must be about now that King

Halfdan hears that his elder brother King Ivar is dead, leaving Barid Ivarson as King of Dublin. Does Halfdan suddenly feel older? Is it time to consolidate?

What happens next looks like a deal between King Halfdan and his Great Army, and King Guthrum and the younger Summer Army: If Guthrum helps Halfdan conquer Mercia, Guthrum can have Essex and East Anglia.

In AD873, King Halfdan storms south into Mercia, and expels King Burgred (who goes off to die in Rome). The Great Heathen Army winters in Repton in central Mercia, well away from the cold east coast this time. Repton is probably a royal centre. It looks as if the Vikings mess up the church there, first incorporating it in fortifications, then turning the Royal Burial ground into a pagan cemetery, complete with human sacrifices.

King Halfdan establishes a buffer zone between Wales and Viking Mercia and gives it to a local lord called Ceolwulf. Ceowulf styles himself "King of the Mercians", complete with coinage and bishops in attendance. King Alfred of Wessex, playing the long game, recognises him.

Now King Halfdan has had enough of the South. In AD875 he returns to Northumberland. He secures his northern border by slaughtering an inordinate number of Picts. Next he heads for Ireland where the descendants of King Ivar and Olaf the White have started feuding.

King Ivar the Boneless had left Olaf the White in place as King of Dublin. However, it was Ivar's son Barid who succeeded him. Perhaps Olaf's son Eystein objected and tried to take the crown. It would certainly explain why King Halfdan slays him.

AD876 finds Halfdan back in Northumberland, sharing out the territory with his veteran followers. The next year he returns to Ireland and fights the Fair Foreigners, those pesky descendants of the first wave of Vikings.

Perhaps Halfdan's just being a good uncle, or perhaps he sees himself as an over-king like Ivar the Boneless. It doesn't matter. In AD877 King Halfdan falls in battle.

Ivar the Boneless's brawling descendants will continue to rule their corner of Ireland on and off into the next century. Another Halfdan – perhaps King Halfdan's son – seems to take over the crown of Yorvic.

But let's go back to AD875. When King Halfdan marches north, King Guthrum leads the younger and hungrier men south for a final showdown with King Alfred.

GUTHRUM vs ALFRED: THE SHOWDOWN

King Guthrum pushes into Wessex. King Alfred confronts him. Rather than fight a battle, they make a peace treaty and exchange hostages. Guthrum cheerfully swears an oath on Christian holy relic to leave the kingdom. Then he mounts a night attack, slays most of Alfred's bodyguard, just misses taking out Alfred, then slips off to the City of Exeter on the south coast of Wessex.

Meanwhile, King Alfred, now approaching his thirties, has been busy. He's brought in Frisian experts to build a navy of big, fat, well manned inshore craft. They're already blooded. Now he uses them to blockade Exeter while he lays siege by land. A massive Viking fleet tries to break the siege. Alfred's fleet send most of them to the bottom.

A second fleet arrives with a similar result, except that the survivors manage to land. However, Alfred chases them to Exeter and forces the whole lot to go back to Mercia; Vikings go home. The next year, AD877, is when King Halfdan dies in Ireland. It's not really clear who's ruling Yorvic. However, whoever it is, King Guthrum isn't scared of this new monarch, so pushes deeper into Mercia and carves the place up between his men.

We can assume that, as always, a show of success – sharing out land to followers – brings in the landless adventurers. In AD878, King Guthrum leads a massively reinforced army into Wessex and King Alfred is reduced to hiding in the Somerset marshes in the western half of Wessex.

There's a legend that Alfred, travelling anonymously, spent the night in a cowherd's cottage and got told off for letting the cakes burn.

However, don't imagine him as a romantic guerrilla leader. The Wessex forces are still organised, just penned in one end of the country. One of Ivar's relatives brings 23 ships, lands behind Alfred's position and lays siege to a coastal fort. The defenders sally out at dawn, catch the Vikings sleeping or hungover and slaughter the chieftain and eight hundred of his men. They gain a vast haul of booty, including a raven banner woven by Ivar's sisters.

By Easter, King Alfred has regrouped. He leads the men of Somerset, Wiltshire and Hampshire to march on the Viking camp at Chippenham.

It looks like King Guthrum rushes out to catch King Alfred in his camp, but is roundly beaten in an awesome clash of armies for which we have no tactical details whatsoever. (Sorry.)

Alfred besieges the Vikings in Chippenham, and after a two week siege they come to terms. Guthrum agrees to be baptised.

King Guthrum and his men can choose a hard life of campaigning, battles and sieges, or they can divide up the land they've already got and live as lords with servants and slaves. Oddly, they choose the latter.

Even so, Alfred still has to defend his kingdom from have-a-go marauders. That autumn, a Viking army sails up Thames, camps near London, but then sits tight for a year, unable to muster up the gumption to actually attack Wessex. A year later and the fleet is off for easier pickings in France. It returns six years later in AD884 and gets a thorough drubbing from the locals. King Alfred and the West Saxons are now properly organised.

So, draw a diagonal line from London up to the top of Wales. All the land above that line belongs to the Vikings. The Anglo-Saxons, who don't much care from which part of Scandinavia the Vikings come from, call it "Danelaw".

Within Danelaw, Guthrum rules East Anglia. A king called Guthrith rules Northumberland. Both are supposed to be Christian. Mercia seems to be a patchwork of Viking chieftains. It's hard to know who they recognise as overlord.

There are still plenty of Anglo-Saxons within Danelaw. The veteran Vikings are lords, not peasant farmers, so the coerls probably barely notice the change of ruler. Not all the English aristocracy are gone, either. They've made common interest with the Vikings and over the generations the distinctions will blur.

Meanwhile, the area below that diagonal line belongs to King Alfred. King Coelwulf, ruler of the Western strip of Mercia next to Wales, dies in AD880 and Alfred puts in his own ealdorman – not a king – to run it. In AD886, Alfred uses a Viking raid as an excuse and grabs London.

And that's the thing. The Vikings have half of England, but Alfred now has all of the unconquered English. The invaders have eaten the rival kingdoms, making the King of Wessex, by default. King of the English.

WHAT HAPPENED NEXT

So we've reached the 880's. A hundred years ago, the Vikings turned up as raiders. The real invasions kicked off only thirty years ago. We saw King Ivar the Boneless, a brutal strategic genius, carve out a Heathen empire stretching from Dublin, through Northumberland, and down to East Anglia. We saw his brother King Halfdan try to take up the reigns, only to get himself killed in Ireland. We saw the young King Guthrum trying to succeed where greater men failed, then sink back into history as a Christian convert ruling a provincial kingdom.

Alfred, ever the geek, tinkers with the balance between his military and economic power. He sets up a network of forts – burghs – to provide secure administrative centres and places of refuge. The rotating garrison system effectively creates the first standing army seen in Britain since the Romans left.

Over the next century, Wessex absorbs Danelaw to form the Kingdom of England proper. Well-organised, rich, and tax-paying, England's strengths also make it a tempting target for more waves of invaders. The last, of course, is the Viking-descended William the Conqueror, Duke of Normandy, who successfully conquers England in AD1066.

Remember that legend that Ivar the Boneless was buried where he could protect England from further invaders? The same legend tells us that William the Conqueror made a point of seeking out Ivar's tomb and very thoroughly burning the old Viking's mummified remains.

Game Over.

AFTERWORD

Thank you for reading *The Official War of the Vikings Game Guide* – we hope you enjoyed it!

Please visit the Paradox Books Facebook page and tell us what you think about the book. You can also follow us on Twitter, and visit our website for a look at our other great book titles.

And you can sign up for our newsletter to stay up to date on all games and books from Paradox Interactive.

Tomas Härenstam
Publishing Director
Paradox Books

OTHER TITLES BY PARADOX BOOKS

Blood in the Streets: A *War of the Roses* Novel

The Sword is Mightier: A *War of the Roses* Novel

The Ninth Element: A *Magicka* Novel

The Dark between the Stars: A *Coriolis* Novel

A Fall of Kings: A *Crusader Kings II* Novel

The Chronicles of Konstantinos:
A *Crusader Kings II* Narrative Guide

One Land, One Faith, One Queen:
A *Europa Universalis IV* Narrative Guide

The Communist Campaign in Karelia:
A *Hearts of Iron III* Strategy Guide

A Year with Mojang: Behind the Scenes of Minecraft

www.paradoxplaza.com/books